Cream Beer

Take 2 oz. of tartaric acid
2 lbs of white sugar and
the juice of half a lemon
and 3 pts. of water, boil
together 5 minutes. when
nearly cold add the whites
of 3 eggs well beaten with half a cup
& half an ounce of essence
of checkerberry.
Bottle and keep in a cool
place, and if very hot
Carbonate of Soda

Mead
2 lbs. G Sugar
½ pt of Molasses.
3 oz. of Tartaric Acid
Essence of Lemon
1 qt of water. Put 2 table
spoonfuls in 1 glass of
water and a quarter spoon
of Soda.
Let stand over night better

This is a reproduction of a page from the original manuscript.

The contents of this book only cover about fifteen years of the original cookbook-journal.

Since this journal is based on the lives of real people the names have been changed.

The Captain's Lady
Cookbook — Personal Journal

Circa: Massachusetts 1837–1917

Edited:

Barbara Dalia Jasmin

The Captain's Lady Collections, Publishers
65-69 High Street
Springfield, Massachusetts 01105

1982

Special thanks to Dover Publications, Inc. in appreciation for the use of material from their pictorial volume of Early Advertising Art.

"Dedication"

To My Captain
Love Is Eternal
*Grá
A Ghrá
A captáen
Stiof'áin ó Diochon

B.D.

"Prayer"

May the bright white shining light of Jesus Christ surround and protect; may the bright green light of health encircle and the bright pink light of love enfold me and everyone I love and all those who touch my life.

Foreword

Several years ago I found the original manuscript for this cookbook-journal. As I read through the handwritten pages of faded copperplate, I felt as if I had stepped back in time to an era of majestic clipper ships, the Civil War, a dashing captain and his lovely lady who awaited her husband's return from sea so many times. As I followed her through those many years of anxiety, I came to know a courageous, devoted, sensitive, caring, warm, loving, educated woman. She spent many hours perfecting a style of cooking we now recognize as "typical" New England.

We read about her family and her husband's family, her deep love for music, poetry, literature and art; her handicrafts, shopping trips, her dog, favourite books — all the intellectual and house-wifely pursuits of an elegant lady of her times — an authentic Gothic heroine — in this instance —

"The Captain's Lady"

B.D.J.

The Captain and I were married March 18, 1857 at the Church of St. Michael by Reverend Father Patrick Stephens —

Today I commence a new life. I shall also start writing my 2nd volume of a personal journal and cookbook. Everything I discover; everyone I love; everything I am interested in will be included. May the Lord bless my Captain and me and my little book.

My Family

Father, Jonathan Augustus Phillips was born	Nov. 10, 1797
Mother, Elizabeth Maria Charles was born	May 8, 1800
Jonathan	July 24, 1823
Dalia	Feb. 26, 1825
Charles Philip	March 26, 1827
Joseph	Nov. 24, 1829
Lucy Elizabeth	Oct. 31, 1831
Virginia May	Sept. 23, 1833
Nicolas Albert	April 19, 1835
Barbara Victoria	Oct. 9, 1837

Mother died 1878, April 5
aged 78.
Father died 1872, Dec. 6
aged 75.
Lucy Elizabeth died 1859, Jan. 25
aged 28.
Charles Philip died March 18, 1857
aged 30 — lost at sea.
Jonathan died December 6, 1860
aged 37 — lost at sea.

My mother and father were both very cultivated, dignified people. My father — a tall, dark, comely man — very loving, kind and judicious. He believed it very important that his daughters be as well educated and accomplished as his sons. I was even instructed in navigation!

Never was there a lovelier, better-bred woman than my mother. She was the mistress of a large well-ordered establishment. She never hurried, was given to great hospitality, tasteful in her dress and also a very fine singer. She expected that my sisters and I would have a great, working knowledge of all household affairs so that we could instruct our help in the correct manner of running a large home. I learned how to keep accurate accounts and personal journals; also to structure my time, my studies and my life in a most satisfying and worthwhile way.

We were also brought up in a loving home with a great and abiding faith in God.

My Nieces and Nephews

Albert Alden Longley and
Virginia May Phillips were
married December 26, 1860

Albert Alden Longley II
born Nov. 24, 1861

Ida Maria Longley
born Jan. 16, 1865

Virginia May Longley
born May 18, 1872

Richard Alden Longley
born August 11, 1875

The Captain's Nieces

Eva Maria Phillips
born August 1, 1855

Jennie Maria Dickson
born April 12, 1853

Carrie Estella Dickson
born January 27, 1856

"My Captain's Family"

Father, Michael Patrick Dickson was born December 21, 1798
Mother, Elizabeth Ann O'Neill   June 13, 1799
Elsbeth Maeve   July 6, 1819
Patrick Joseph   July 9, 1821
Anna Maria   March 24, 1823
Michael George   March 13, 1825
Stephen Patrick   June 3, 1831
Ann Dorothea   March 16, 1833

Mother died 1879, Sept. 11
aged 80
Father died 1880, Sept. 13
aged 81
Anna Maria died 1861, Feb. 14
aged 37
Elsbeth Maeve died 1866, June 19
aged 47

○────∞∞∞〉✶

All that I have written about my family can again be expressed for my Captain's family. 'Tis truly said that when a man finds a woman who is surrounded by the same marvelous atmosphere that contains all the good things of life like joy, love, peace, he is enchanted. He has not only fallen in love but has found a safe harbour in which together they will be safe from all the vicissitudes of life.

○────∞∞∞〉✶

My Captain's Favourite Poem —

"Come my friends,
'Tis not too late to seek a newer world.
Push off, and sitting well in order smite
The sounding furrows; for my purpose holds
To sail beyond the sunset and the baths
Of all the western stars, until I die.
It may be that the gulfs will wash us down:
It may be we shall touch the Happy Isles,
And see the Great Achilles, whom we knew.
Though much is taken, much abides and though
We are not now that strength which in old days
Moved earth and heaven, that which we are, we are —
One equal temper of heroic hearts,
Made weak by time and fate, but strong in will
To strive, to seek, to find, and not to yield.

"Ulysses" Alfred, Lord Tennyson

"The Way of Life"
6th Century B.C. Chinese

He who is open-eyed is open-minded.
He who is open-minded is open-hearted.
He who is open-hearted is Kingly.
He who is Kingly is godly,
He who is godly is useful.
He who is useful is infinite.
He who is infinite is immune.
He who is immune is immortal.

"It is necessary to do right; it is not necessary to be happy. However, when we do right, we find happiness."

"Mrs. Brigham's Sauce"

Take one quart of molasses. Boil 10 or 15 minutes. Add 3 well beaten eggs slowly. After a few minutes, add extract of lemon.

———

"Cottage Pudding"

Stir well together 1 pint of flour; 1 teaspoonful butter; 2 eggs; 1 teaspoonful soda; 2 teaspoonsful cream tartar and 1 teacup of fresh, sweet milk. Put into a deep pan & bake half an hour. Serve with sauce made to the taste.

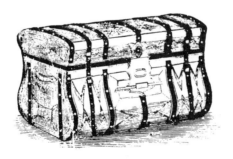

The Captain brought me a hand-carved hope chest from the Orient for my 16th birthday. We also pledged our troth that day. Since then I have been filling it with so many beautiful things, I am afraid I will need a second chest by the time the wedding takes place.

"The Wedding"

March 18, 1857

It is a soft, misty, early spring day. The sky is blue, the sun is bright. There seems to be a special radiance wherever I look. I feel that I am walking through a dream. I am now dressed in my beautiful, soft white gown of O'Callaghan lace over tissue taffeta with a myriad of petticoats to make it stand out. My Captain brought the materials from Ireland along with a very special bouquet of white silk Killarney roses: My Golden Celtic Cross and my Claddagh wedding ring he brought back on his last voyage. My long, French illusion veil is caught up with the same roses and looks very pretty against my light auburn hair done up in large curls and waves. My father brought my pearls from the Orient several years ago.

My bridesmaids — my sisters, sisters-in-law and cousins — look like a veritable rainbow in every shade imaginable — blues, greens, pinks, violet. My little nieces are dressed in white replicas of my gown.

I arrived at St. Michael's Church in our large carriage with my father and mother. They looked at me so lovingly and proud. We then all arranged ourselves in a procession; the music started and I, leaning on my father's arm, walked down the long aisle to the altar. There he stood — My Captain — tall, blond, bearded, handsome, strong, honest and true. The Mass was very special, the music lovely. We made our pledges to each other and sealed them with a kiss. Then we turned and started down the aisle to be greeted by our relatives and friends. May the happiness, beauty and sanctity of this moment never cease. I fervently believe that "Love is Eternal." May God bless us both and may his bright, shining light of love encircle and protect us forever.

Amen.

"How Do I Love Thee?"
Elizabeth Barrett Browning

How do I love thee? Let me count the ways,
I love thee to the depth and breadth and height
My soul can reach when feeling out of sight
For the ends of Being and ideal Grace.
I love thee to the level of every day's
Most quiet need, by sun and candle-light.
I love thee freely, as men strive for Right.
I love thee purely, as they turn from Praise,
I love thee with the passion put to use
In my old griefs, and with my childhood's faith.
I love thee with a love I seemed to lose
With my lost saints — I love thee with the breath
Smiles, tears, of all my life! — and, if God choose
I shall but love thee better after death.

"Bachelor Cake"

1 lb. flour, ½ lb. sugar, ½ lb. butter, ½ lb. currants and sultanas*, grated nutmeg, 1 teaspoonful ground ginger, 1 teaspoonful cinnamon, 1 teaspoonful baking powder, 4 eggs, ½ teacupful boiling sweet milk. Rub butter into the flour, add all the other ingredients. Mix with well-beaten eggs and as much milk as will make the whole into a smooth mixture. Bake in a moderate oven about 2 hours.

My heart is like a singing bird
Whose nest is in a water'd shoot;
My heart is like an apple tree
Whose boughs are bent with thick-set fruit;
My heart is like a rainbow shell
That paddles in a halycon sea;
My heart is gladder than all these,
Because my love is come to me.

Christina Rossetti

* See appendix.

"Groom's Cake"

2 cups butter
1 lb. Barbados sugar*
18–20 eggs large-size
½ cup Devonshire cream
3 teaspoonsful baking powder
1 cup brandy
1 tablespoonful extract of orange
2 lbs. currants
2 lbs. sultanas
2 lbs. seeded raisins
1½ lbs. citron
4½ cups flour
2 teaspoonsful cinnamon
1 tablespoonful nutmeg
1 tablespoonful allspice
1½ cups slivered, blanched almonds

Cream butter and sugar. Beat eggs and add; then add liquids. Sift flour and spices over fruit. Blend the two mixtures and fill several baking pans nearly to top (lined with buttered and floured paper). Bake in a slow oven about 3 hours or steam three hours and bake one hour. Cool, ice and store in tins. Every now and then saturate with 1½ cups more brandy.

"English Plum Cake"

½ lb. flour
6 oz. butter
6 oz. Barbados sugar
6 oz. Sultanas, dredged in flour
6 eggs, med. size
4 tablespoonsful cream
glace cherries
1 tablespoonful vinegar
1 large tablespoonful of molasses
a touch of salt and baking powder

Cream eggs and butter; add each ingredient to mixture; beat well. Bake about an hour in a hot oven then little by little cool to medium heat.

Thy husband is thy lord, thy life, thy keeper,
Thy head, thy sovereign; one that cares for thee.
And for thy maintenance; commits his body
To painful labour both by sea and land,
To watch the night in storms, the day in cold,
Whilst thou li'st warm at home, secure and safe.

"Matrimonial Cakes"

Make a crumbly dough of the following: 1 ½ cups oatmeal; 1 ½ cups flour; 1 cup brown sugar; ¾ cup lard; ½ teaspoonful baking soda and ¼ teaspoonful salt. Spread one half of mixtures on long, flat baking sheet. Make filling of 8 oz. dates; juice of ½ lemon; ½ cup of sugar; ½ tsp. salt and ½ cup water. Cook ingredients for 5 min.; stir and cool. Spread filling on dough and cover with the rest of the dough. Bake in medium oven until lightly browned.

"For I in thy heart had dwelling and thou hast in mine forever.

"Bride's Cake"

3 cups sifted flour
5 tablespoonsful baking powder
1/2 teaspoonful salt
1 cup butter
2 cups castor* sugar
1/2 tsp. extract of rosé*
1 tsp. extract of almond
1 cup sweet milk
6 whites of large fresh eggs

Sift dry ingredients several times, cream butter and sugar well. Add extracts and milk together then add to flour mixture. Beat egg whites and fold in. Turn all into greased Turk's Head cake pan* and bake in moderate oven for 1 1/2 hours.

My bounty is as boundless as the sea, my love as deep; the more I
    give to thee,
The more I have, for both are infinite.

"Romeo and Juliet"

* See appendix.

"A Worthy Wife"

When one finds a worthy wife, her value is far beyond pearls.
Her husband, entrusting his heart to her has an unfailing prize.
She brings him good, and not evil, all the days of her life.
She obtains wool and flax and makes cloth with skillful hands.
She puts her hands to the distaff, and her fingers ply the spindle.
She reaches out her hands to the poor, and extends her arms to the needy.
Charm is deceptive and beauty fleeting; the woman who fears the
   Lord is to be praised.
Give her a reward of her labors, and let her works praise her at the
   city gates.

This is the true measure of love, when we believe that we alone
can love, that no one could ever have loved so before us, and that no
one will ever love in the same way after us.

von Goethe

"Great Ladies"

After my mother and mother-in-law and my great Aunt Victoria,
I admire Queen Victoria and Jenny Lind, the famous singer, the
most. They are all women of intellect, integrity, energy, stead-
fastness and godliness who use their varied positions in life to set an
estimable example for women-in-general and me in particular to
follow. How fortunate I am to be living in these enlightened times
of great progress and high esteem for women. To be admired and
treated as an equal in all manner of intellectual pursuits by my
husband — I am, truly, a fortunate woman.

"Household & Wedding"
"Goods & Presents"

1. Hand carved teak wood hope chest filled with beautiful bed-linens, towels, tablecloths, lace cloths, tea cloths, softest of pure woolen blankets in all shades of lovely colors. A trousseau of the loveliest Irish lace-trimmed gowns and peignors.

2. Service for 24 — Spode — rose pattern from England Daily service — Willow Ware

3. Service of all types of glassware — Waterford — Crystal — Ireland. 24 of each size glass.

4. Service of sterling silver flatware — 24 place setting, a rose pattern.

5. A new Swedish stove. My cook, Ayuh, is extremely proficient in its use.

6. Handelian lamps, Waterford Crystal lamps, cut-glass lamps.

7. Sterling silver English tea service with tray.

8. Sterling silver, trays, salver, épérgné, candelabra, candlesticks, castor set, syrup pitcher, chocolate set, tureen, plates, decanters, etc.

9. Cut glassware of every kind.

10. Canopied bed — so beautiful — designed of teak wood carved by a very skilled artisan. For the spring I will have all muslin trimmed with lace probably white and in winter rose brocade.

11. Wash sets in wild rose pattern.

12. Bread plates, bride's baskets.

13. Shamrock tea set.

14. Beleek pieces from Ireland.

15. Fireplace accessories.

16. Paintings

17. Cake dishes and cake stands.

18. Quilts.

19. Magnificent spreads and drapes.

20. Tea wagon.

21. Grandfather's clock.

22. Melodian.

23. Grand piano and so much more.

"Simnel Cake"

6 oz. butter, ½ lb. flour, 2 eggs, 2 oz. chopped mixed peel, 1 teaspoonful baking powder, almond paste, 6 oz. castor sugar, ¼ lb. currants.

Beat butter and sugar to a cream then add eggs and dry ingredients alternately. Add baking powder. Butter a round cake tin and put in half of the cake mixture. Smooth then cover with a layer of half of the almond paste. Add the remainder of the cake mixture. Bake for 1½ hours in a moderate oven. When done turn out and cool. Brush the surface of the cake with a layer of almond paste. Smooth it round the sides and over the top with a knife. Either leave plain or decorate with blanched almonds.

To be served Easter Sunday.

"I know that my Redeemer Liveth."

"Suet Pudding"
or
"English Roly-Poly"

1 cup molasses
1 cup raisins
1 cup chopped suet
1 cup sour milk
2 eggs

1 good teaspoonful mixed of the following: soda, mace*, cloves, cassia*, nutmeg and add flour enough to make a good batter. Steam 3–4 hours.

June 3, 1857

The Captain's birthday — 26th

The Captain's father together with my father have just launched the new clipper ship, "The Golden Fleece." The Captain takes command two months after the wedding at the end of May. He sails around the Horn to Calcutta and will be gone for many, many long months. I would choose to wait for him rather than for any other man in the entire world.

* See appendix.

"My Brother, Charles"

August 22, 1857

Word has just been received today of the death at sea of my dearest brother Charles Philip. He was Captain of the tall, square rigger "The Valiant" that went down with all souls aboard on my wedding day, March 18, 1857.

I remember him so vividly a great, big powerful man with black curly hair and beard, a soft, laughing look to his eye and the scent of the sea and English lavender always about him. He had a wry grin and always let me fill his Irish clay pipe with aromatic Turkish tobacco. Then he'd puff away as I excitedly told him about my dreams, plans and fancies. He used to bring me back dolls and pretty things to wear from all his many voyages around the world.

I think before he left this time he had a premonition of impending disaster because he asked me to take care of his dog, King, a big fawn-colored shepherd.

I remember now so vividly the day of my wedding. As I was just about to enter the carriage, King suddenly started to bark joyfully and ran to the gates, prancing about all the way back to me as if he saw someone I did not. Then, as my father assisted me into the carriage I felt a light touch on my face and then King sat down very still at my feet, head on paws and refused to move. I let him be and when we got to the Church he stood guard until my Captain and I came out together. Then he took up his position at my Captain's feet. He must have known then that his old master would never return again.

○━━━━✕

"Lines"

Farewell, dear friends in Christ below
I bid you all a short adieu
My time is come, I long to go
To Heaven my Saviour's face to view.
I thank you for your kindness shown
My Jesus will reward you all
I leave you with the Lord alone
And safely in his arms I fall.
Farewell dear neighbors, brethren, friends,
I hope we soon shall meet with joy;
My heavenly Father for me sends,
I go where nothing can annoy.
Adieu to all things here below,
Vain world, I leave thy fleeting toys.
Adieu to sin, fear, pain and woe,
And welcome bright eternal joys.
Temptations, troubles, griefs, adieu
Sorrows becloud my face no more;
I go to pleasure ever new:
Where trial, and strife, and wars are o'er.
Now I have done with earthly things
And all to come is boundless bliss
My eager spirit spreads her wings
Jesus says — I answer yes.
Weep not dear friends — I tell you all
I go to dwell with Christ on high

I hear my blessed Saviour's call
And trusting in his promise; die.

Verses written by Jane A. Wyler before she drowned herself
April 11, 1858.

Hours we once enjoyed together have passed away,
The memory of Thee will ever be among my happiest recollections.

We meet but to part; though we part here, may we meet again in
that world of fadeless joy.

There is nothing true but Heaven.

"Cousin Jane"

Yes! O yes Cousin Jane, thy name be,
A rosy wreathe will I twine for thee?
Although far distant on the earth's brow,
Beneath the lofty tree's drooping bough,
Dost thou remember our pleasant stroll,
O'er Soukegan bridge, and Goldsmith's knoll,
We tracked the wood paths through the pathless wood,
To where the dwellings of our kindred stood.
Sweet friend! Pleasant times have passed quite,
Since thy young form vanished from my sight.
Still my heart with thy glad smiles is bright
Far in the woodland green and dreamy light.
Bright eyes and rosy lips 'dorn thy face,
Reverence and modesty thy grace,
I trust that all with Jane is well
'Tis a bitter word to say Farewell.

B.V. Dickson

"Dear Jane"

May the hand of Providence ever deal gently with thee. And may the gates of plenty and happiness ever be open to thee and thine. May no rude blast disturb the harmony of thy existence, But like a gentle river, may thy life flow smoothly on till it is peacefully lost in the great ocean of eternity. Accept these few lines as a token of remembrance,

From your Friend,
A.J.W.

I would that life might be to thee
A sunny path from sorrow free
A gentle stream to bear thee o'er
Life's billows to a brighter shore.
May loving friends to thee be given
To bear thee on the way to Heaven.

The wish of your friend,
Carrie

"Cousin Jane Wyler"

Cousin Jane Wyler was laid to rest today in a forgotten lichen-covered, maple-shaded corner of the old Protestant church-yard. The beauty of the early spring day enhanced by the sweet fragrances wafting up from the deep masses of varigated lilacs and snowy white syringia only seemed to intensify the poignancy of her tragic demise. If only I could have helped sustain her in her sorrow, anguish and shame, dissuaded her from engaging in self-condemnation. But, alas! To no avail. She said, "I can bear any physical pain stoically, but not the soul-searing pain of watching the disappointment and disgust in the innocent eyes of my family and friends. Worst of all to be denied worship and the Sacraments in my Church. I neither seek nor desire pity. I have searched my soul and my eyes are blinded with tears for my beloved Jonathan and the loss of my honor. I cannot live without respect and honor. Death would be a welcome friend and companion. Then my loneliness and self-imposed exile would be ended. My Jesus awaits His recalcitrant and penitent child."

I tried to persuade her to journey to friends in Prescott in the western part of the state. They would have shielded her in her time of travail; but, she would hear none of it. She deemed it just and proper to pay for her sinful behaviour in full measure. If only her betrothed had not died one week before the wedding at New Year's. I fear that Cousin Jane with her great religious fervour and refined and delicate sensibilities, had descended into melancholia and morbidity and, therefore, must needs censure herself far beyond society's monumental demands. Her guilt became for her an emotional obsession that naught could ever change. I pray that

Our Saviour, in His Infinite love and wisdom, will join them together as one forever on high.

Jane and Jonathan
and their unborn

"May a rosy wreathe entwine them for all eternity."

April 11, 1858

He who binds to himself a joy
Does the winged life destroy;
But he who kisses the joy as it flies
Lives in Eternity's sunrise.

"Cream Sponge Cake No. 1"

Mrs. Ames Marriott

Beat 6 eggs 2 minutes.
Add 3 cups of fine white sugar.
Beat 5 minutes.
2 cups of flour 2 teaspoonsful cream of tartar
Beat 2 minutes.
1 teaspoonful soda in one cup cold water
Beat 1 minute.
Add the juice 1 lemon or ½ rind grated.
2 cups flour
Beat 1 minute.

Observe this rule exactly and bake in two deep pans in a medium oven for precisely 1 hour.

I am cross-stitching a new sampler — Faith, Hope and Charity.

Very nice but <u>very tedious.</u>

From the Canterbury Tales

"A Knyght"

Geoffrey Chaucer

A Knyght there was and that a worthy man,
Who, from the moment when he first began
To ride forth, loved the code of chivalry:
Honor and truth, freedom and courtesy.
His lord's war had established him in worth;
He rode — and no man further — ends of earth.
In heathen parts as well as Christendom,
Honored wherever he might go or come.
Of mortal battles he had seen fifteen,
And fought hard for our faith at Tramassene
Thrice in the lists, and always slain his foe.
This noble knight was even led to go
To Turkey, where he fought most valiantly
Against the heathen hordes for Palaty
Renowned he was; and, worthy, he was wise —
Prudence, with him, was more than mere disguise;
He was as meek in manner as a maid.
Vileness he shunned, rudeness he never said
In all his life, respecting each man's right
He was a truly perfect noble knyght.

"My Captain"

28

"Washington Pie Cake"

1 ½ cups flour
1 cup sugar
2/3 cups milk
2 eggs
butter the size of an egg
2/3 teaspoon cream tartar
1/3 soda
Bake 40–45 min. in a medium oven.

Filling for Pie

1 egg; the juice of one lemon and a little extra of lemon.
1 tablespoonful corn starch; boil in 1 cup of water; 1 cup of sugar.

To prepare this, boil the cornstarch in a cup of water, then add the other ingredients and boil all together thoroughly cooking the whole. Cool before adding to the pie-cake. Cut pie-cake in 2 layers and fill with lemon custard. Frost with chocolate.

"Hold close
with open hands."

May 1st

'Tis Mayday at last. The spring is come and cold winter's winds have ceased for awhile, praise God! In accordance with the olden rites, huge bonfires have been blazing on the hilltops since before dawn to honor the return of the sun and its welcome warmth. On the village green a Maypole has been placed for the boys and girls to dance around later in the day. I think I will go into our woods and gather some branches of May. Our woods are so lovely and always seem filled with a deep peace. At this early hour, the birches, oaks and maples will be silvery with morning dew. There will be slight stirrings of unseen wild things and the rustle of wings to be heard but their sound will only serve to intensify the deep stillness.

"Now is the month of Maying where merry lads are playing."

"Date-Nut Squares"

Mrs. Waltham

Beat 4 eggs; add 1 cup of sugar; 1½ teaspoonsful vanilla; 1 cup flour; 1 teaspoonful baking powder; 1 teaspoonful salt; 2 cups nuts; 4 cups chopped-up dates rolled in flour. Press batter into a greased pan and put into a slow oven about ½ hour. Cut up in pieces, roll in powdered sugar.

"On May Morning"

John Milton

Now the bright morning Star, Daye's harbinger,
Comes dancing from the East, and leads with her
The Flowery May, who from her green lap throws
The yellow Cowslip, and the pale Primrose,
Hail, bounteous May! that dost inspire
Mirth, and youth, and warm desire;
Woods and Groves are of thy dressing;
Hill and Dale doth boast thy blessing;
Thus we salute thee with our early Song
And welcome thee, and wish thee long.

"Date-Nut Cake"

Mrs. Malcolm Carlyle

Add 4 teaspoonsful baking powder to 4 tablespoonsful flour;
1/4 teaspoonful salt; 1 1/2 cups bread crumbs or stale cake crumbs;
cream 1/4 cup butter to 1 1/8 cups loaf sugar; 3 eggs; 1 teaspoonful
vanilla; 1 1/2 cup chopped and pitted dates; 1 1/2 cups nuts; 1 1/4
cups sweet milk. Pour into a long cake mold and bake in a slow
oven for 50–60 minutes.

"From the Romantic Age"

All in the blue unclouded weather
Thick-jewelled shone the saddle leather
The helmet and the helmet feather
Burnied like one burning flame together
As he rode down to Camelot.

31

'Graham Bread"

Mrs. Stone's receipt

Make a batter of milk and water, flour and yeast, a pinch of salt. Let it rise very light. Then add molasses and graham flour enough to mold. Let it rise, then bake.

"French Cake"

Mrs. Samuel Farnsworth's receipt

1 cup milk
3 eggs
½ cup butter
2 cups sugar
3 cups flour
2 teaspoonsful cream of tartar
  teaspoonful soda

Bake about 40–50 minutes in a moderate oven.

"Hermits"

Mrs. Bachelder & Mrs. Stone
"very nice"

1½ cup sugar
⅔ cup butter
2 eggs
1 teaspoonful soda
dissolved in 2 tablespoonful milk, 1 teaspoonful nutmeg; 1
teaspoonful cloves; 1 teaspoonful cinnamon and salt.
1 cup chopped raisins
Flour enough to roll hard.
Bake in medium oven about 20–25 minutes.

"Superior"

"Cornwall Buns"

Aunt Alba's receipt

3 cups milk
1 cup sugar
1 cup yeast made into sponge
In the morning add another cup of sugar.
1 cup butter
1 teaspoonful of soda
Bake in medium oven about 15–20 minutes.

"Excellent Johnny Cake"

take one quart of milk
3 eggs
1 teaspoonful saleratus
1 teacup wheat flour and Indian meal sufficient to make a batter of the consistency of pancakes.

"Never fear to speak what is in your heart."

"Parker House Rolls"

Mrs. Brigham's

2 quarts of flour
1 pint of scalded milk
½ cup sugar
½ cup yeast

One spoonful of lard stirred into the flour when you commence. Make a hole in the middle of the flour and stir in sugar, yeast, milk and a little salt. Let stand until morning, then stir it up and let it rise 'til 3 o'clock. Stir it up and roll in butter and cut out and fold together. Let rise, then bake about 15 minutes in a medium hot oven.

"Very nice"

A glorious day! A June day! The Captain puts into port today!

his birthday, June 3rd

o—◦◦◦◦◦◦◦✕

"Rich Loaf Cake"

1 cup of butter
1½ cup sugar
4 eggs
½ cup milk both fresh and sweet
3 cups prepared flour
½ cup molasses
2 cups chopped raisins
1 teaspoonful cloves
1 teaspoonful cinnamon
½ teaspoonful nutmeg
½ cup citron cut up
baking soda
Bake from 1–1½ hours in a moderate oven.

Frost if you wish.
_____

1 pint cream cheese
1 pound powdered sugar
½ teaspoon salt
4 tablespoons thick cream
1 teaspoonful vanilla

o—◦◦◦◦◦◦◦✕

"Scripture Cake"

Ladies of the Church

3½ cups — 1st Kings iv:22 (flour)

1 cup — Judges v:25 (butter)

2 cups — Jeremiah vi: 20 (sugar)

2 cups — I Samuel xxx:12 (sultanas)

2 cups — Nahum iii:12 (figs)

2 cups — Numbers xvii:8 (almonds)

2 tablespoonsful Amos iv:5 (saleratus*)

¼ tablespoonful Leviticus ii:12 (salt)

6 Jeremiah xvii:11 (eggs)

2 tablespoonsful 1st Samuel xiv:25 (honey)

½ cup Judges iv:19 (sweet milk)

Season to taste with 2nd Chronicles ix:9 (spices)

Add citron

Mix altogether; beat well.

Place in slow oven 1½ to 2 hours.

Mix altogether; beat well. Place in greased and floured pan then place in slow oven 1½ to 2 hours.

"Elizabethan Song"

Spring, the year's spring, is the year's pleasant king;
Then blooms each thing, then maids dance in a ring;
Cold doth not sting the pretty birds do sing,
Cuckoo, jug-jug pu-wee to witta-woo.

* See appendix.

"Mrs. Spaulding's Shortcake"

3 cups flour
½ tsp. salt
4 teaspoonsful baking powder
½ cup sugar
½ cup lard
1 ¼ cups sweet, fresh milk
1 large egg, beaten

Mix altogether until all flour is moistened, put in large baking pan and sprinkle with sugar. Bake 15 minutes in a hot oven. Roll out lightly if little cakes are desired. Pour on top a little melted butter either way. Cut and place on a flat sheet. Serve with crushed, sweetened strawberries. Cover with sweetened, frothy cream. It is delicious.

"California Cake"

2 cups sugar
1 cup water
1 cup butter
3 cups of flour
2 eggs
½ teaspoonful soda
1 teaspoon of cream of tartar
Bake about 45–50 minutes in a medium oven.

"*Those only are happy who have their minds fixed on some object other than their own happiness; on the happiness of others, on the improvement of mankind, even on some art or pursuit, followed not as a means, but as itself an ideal end. Aiming thus at something else, they find happiness by the way.*"

— John Stuart Mill —

"*Veal Soup*"

3 lbs. of veal
¼ lb. of salt pork cut very fine
mix in 2 eggs
1 cup pounded crackers
3 teaspoonsful salt and
3 teaspoonsful of pepper and a little mace or nutmeg

Press very hard into a pan and bake ½ hour; cut up in thin slices and eat cold.

"*Different*"

"Curing Beef — Veal"

5 lbs. sugar
5 lbs. salt
5 oz. soda
3 gallons water

This is quantity for 100 lbs. beef or veal. This brine will not keep long in warm weather but in cold it is first rate.

"The Secret of the Sea"
Henry Wadsworth Longfellow

Ah! what pleasant visions haunt me
As I gaze upon the sea!
All the old romantic legends,
All my dreams come back to me.
Sails of silk and ropes of sandal,
Such as gleam in ancient lore;
And the singing of the sailors,
And the answer from the shore.
In each sail that skims the horizon,
In each landward-blowing breeze,
I behold that stately galley,
Hear those mournful melodies;
Till my soul is full of longing
For the secret of the sea,
And the heart of the great ocean
Sends a thrilling pulse through me.

"We sing to Thee, whose wisdom formed
The curious organ of the ear,
And Thou who gavest voices, Lord,
Our grateful songs in kindness hear."

"Prune Duff"

4 eggs
1 cup Barbados brown sugar
½ cup sweet butter
1 ⅓ cup cooked pitted prunes
1 cup flour
½ tsp. salt
1 tsp. soda
1 tsp. sweet milk

Mix and pour in pudding mold. Cover and steam for 1 hour. Serve with sauce — 2 cups prune juice; 2 tablespoonsful lemon juice; 1 tablespoonful butter; 1 ¼ tsp. nutmeg; 3 tablespoonsful cornstarch; ⅔ cup sugar; cook over low heat. Pour over Duff.

"Land's End Fruit Cake"

Mrs. Wendell Warren
West Mednay

1 cup molasses
½ cup butter
2 eggs
½ teaspoon soda
spices of all kinds
1 cup currants
1 cup sultanas
¼ lb. citron
Bake about 1 hour in a medium oven.

"Very Nice"

"Sugar Cookies"

2 cups sugar
1 cup butter
½ cup of cream
1 teaspoonful saleratus *
2 eggs

Bake on greased cookie sheet in a medium oven 10–12 minutes or until done.

Conundrums "Humour"

When is music like vegetables?
Answer: When there are two beats in a measure!

What vice is that which the worst people shun most?
Answer: Advice.

Why are ladies generally bad gramarians?
Answer: Because few of them are able to decline matrimony.

The most impudent of all things is a mirror for it is continually casting reflections.

What key opens the gate to misery?
Answer: Whiskey.

Why does an angry man resemble a lady in full dress?
Answer: Because he is much-ruffled.

"Hope On"

Let us hope on, for whatsoever our lot
However rough the path we have to tread
We never by our Father are forgot
Some blessings upon our pathway shed.
The sky above may show no trace of blue
And gathering clouds may darker still appear
We'll yet hope on some star will struggle through
To show us that a brighter hour is near.
God never makes our lot quite desolate
He leaves some hope, some joy to cheer us on
Leaving us still to strive with adverse fate
To trust His love when much we loved is gone.
Let us be resolute what e'er betide.
Earnest the path of duty to pursue;
And looking ever to the brightest side
Unto our God, ourselves, our friends be true.

B.V. Dickson

"Dandy Pudding"

Mrs. Brigham's

Boil one quart of milk. While boiling, add the beaten yolks of 4 eggs. Two large tablespoonsful of cornstarch. Add ½ cup sugar; salt. After cooking a few minutes pour in a dish. It must be stirred while cooking. Then beat the whites with half a cup of sugar. Pour over the top and bake to a delicate brown.

"Follow the Gleam"

Not of the sunlight,
Not of the moonlight
Not of the starlight!
O young Mariner,
Down to the haven,
Call your companions,
Launch your vessel,
And crowd your canvas,
And ere it vanishes
Over the margin,
After it, follow it,
Follow the Gleam.

"Hoosier Cakes"

1 quart flour
1 teaspoonful cream of tartar
½ teaspoon of soda

Add about 2 cups of sweet milk or enough to moisten like biscuit dough. Roll out the dough about the thickness of a thick pie; you must spread it with thin layer of butter and cover with white sugar. Roll over and over as hard as possible, then cut it off any size you wish, as you would pastry, pinching one end and flouring. Place the end in the pan that has been splattered with butter.

"For Washington Pies"

1 heaping cup butter
5 cups of flour
4 eggs
1 cup milk
1 little nutmeg, fresh ground
2½ cups sugar
1 teaspoonful of soda

Sufficient for 4 pies. Bake in a medium oven 50–60 minutes. Cut into layers and fill with custard. Ice with chocolate.

She walks in beauty like the night
   of cloudless climes and starry skies;
And all that's best of dark and bright
   Meet in her aspect and her eyes:
Thus mellow'd to that tender light
   Which heaven to gaudy day denies.

Lord Byron

"Delicate Tea Cake"

Mrs. Alfrieda Bell

2 cups sugar
½ cup butter
2 eggs
1 cup fresh new milk
4 cups flour
2 teaspoonsful cream tartar
½ teaspoonful soda
1½ teaspoonsful extract of lemon

When cool sprinkle with icing sugar. Bake about 40–50 minutes in a moderate oven.

A thing of beauty is a joy forever;
It's loveliness increases; it will
Never pass into nothingness; but still will keep
A bower quiet for us, and a sleep
Full of sweet dreams, and health and quiet breathing.

John Keats

46

"Parting"

My Captain always felt that it was bad luck to say goodbye when he was about to leave for a voyage — especially a very long one. We were both filled with unspeakable anguish as the time of parting drew near. I knew when the day arrived, however, because he would say to me in a very fortuitous way, "I think I shall sail across the Bay but I shall be back in time for a piece of your special lemon pie." He then held me close, kissed me quickly, turned and was gone. My eyes followed his stalwart figure until he was out of sight. Then — and only then — did I permit the tears to fall. Throughout the long months of waiting I held that picture of him close to my heart. I prayed each day that God would bring him safely home to me once more.

When his return was imminent, I would make a lemon pie almost every day. I really became quite proficient at it. Then, that special day arrived.

My Captain would stride through the door, blue eyes sparkling in his tanned face, his hair and beard a mass of tangled golden curls — I would have the pleasure of trimming them later. He would pick me up, swing me around, hold me so close (I could feel his heart beat!) and say playfully, "Well, my Lady, isn't that lemon pie ready yet?"

"Oyster Pie"

Cover the bottom of the dish with half crackers. Put in a layer of oysters with pepper and salt and butter for seasoning. Continue to do the same till you have it as deep as you wish. Pour over the whole a half-cup or whole one of cream or milk. Cover with pastry and bake. Lobster meat, clams or other pieces of fish may be substituted.

"Beef Steak Cakes"

Take lean, raw beef; chop fine, add chopped onion; pepper and salt to season; bind with an egg; make into small cakes; dip in flour; fry in hot lard or butter.

Dickson, Phillips and Sons
Mercantile Establishment
Shipping Cargoes around the World
Export — Established 1823 — Import
Boston, Mass.

After the Captain returned from his first trip around the Horn, he surprised me with a visit to one of the largest warehouses along the water where our fathers conduct a very profitable shipping and importing business. I was so excited, and in honour of the visit I wore a China silk dress of sea-green with a pure white shawl of Indian cashmere.

As soon as we entered, the strange, fragrant aromas of the orient assailed our nostrils. It was really as if we had stepped into another world. There was box after box with my name carefully stencilled on the top. I could barely wait until the men prised them open. It was a veritable treasure trove.

I am going to enumerate each and everything I received. It actually took several visits for me to see everything and several more days before everything was safely home. My Captain was so proud and happy to delight me so with these tokens of his affection.

List

1. Teas — Lapsing Souchong
   Assam Pekoe
   Jasmine
   Rare Amkoe
   Scented Caper

2. Chinese lanterns — all shapes and sizes — also fancy kites

Perfumes — Attar of Roses
             Musk
             Orange Blossom
             Gardenia
             Jasmine

4. China silks, brocades, Crêpe de Chine, yards and yards!

5. Quassia* cup of wood.

6. Elegant Cheval looking glass.

7. Wines

8. Herb pillow from India filled with saffron, poppies and soothing plants.

9. Turkish sashes, slippers, fancy candies.

10. Bamboo chairs, tables for the porches.

11. A pair of ancient brass andirons.

12. Japanese screens.

13. Wind chimes to catch the breezes.

14. Necklaces, earrings, bracelets, brooches of amber, coral, pearls, lapis lazuli, filigree and opals.

15. Necklace, earrings, bracelets and rings of Jade. The colour of my eyes I think. "True," says the Captain.

16. A beautiful hand-carved chest to match the one I already have. This I will use for the Captain's personal mementos.

17. Incenses of many fragrances — Musk, Sandalwood, Pine and Jasmine.

18. Rose famille set of dishes, every piece imaginable and some I didn't even know existed. Beautiful.

19. A huge China closet of mahogany, Georgian style to hold it all. I really don't know who will reach up to the top shelf. It must be 9 feet tall and 7 feet wide.

20. Yards upon yards, bolt and tube of pure silk brocades and fine silk in eggshell colour for curtains and drapes throughout the entire house. Set against the walnut wainscotting in the house they will look very elegant.

21. A gorgeous brocaded throw for the Grand Piano.

22. Spices: all kinds. Pepper right from Sumatra with a little grinder.

23. Candlesticks of brass.

24. Fireplace fans and implements for several rooms.

25. A huge and varied shell collection. Fascinating. I shall catalog them for the Captain next winter.

26. Brussells lace.
Honitan lace.
Italian laces.
Simply yards of it.

27. Turkish, Oriental carpets: U-Shak for my walnut gate-leg table in the library.
Serapi

Aubusson
Samarkand
Bakhshoish Herati

One more gorgeous than the other. A rose coloured one
for our bedroom. I shall have to decide where they will all go.

o———ᴐᴖᴖᴖᴖ⬧

"Ah, moon of my delight that knows no wane."

Rubiyat

o———ᴐᴖᴖᴖᴖ⬧

"Irish Potatoe Pudding"

Mash about 1 lb. of new hot potatoes until smooth. Add 4 eggs:
1½ cups butter; 1 cup floured sultanas; 2 cups sugar; ½ cup
mixed spices: cloves, cinnamon, allspice and nutmeg; ½ cup
sherry; ½ cup of brandy. Turn mixture into a baking dish lined
with pie pastry and bake in a hot oven for 10 minutes and medium
heat for 30 more or until center is set when knife cuts through
cleanly.

o———ᴐᴖᴖᴖᴖ⬧

July 19, 1858

Our first dinner party was very well received. Everything was
tasteful and correct. The house looked lovely, the food was
pronounced superior. The main course was a "Baron de Boëuf."
Naturally, all the desserts were the Captain's favourites. The
music was excellent. The Captain and I danced the German, the
Waltz, the Lancers and the Redowa. My gown was pale leaf green
tissue silk and French illusion looped with sprays of pale pink silk
roses.

"Shopping"

Essence of Checkerberry *
Tartaric acid *
cakes of unsweetened chocolate
3 cards of isinglas
matches
extracts
sugar
chocolate
tooth powder
combs
flour
tapioca
spices
cream of tartar
baking powder
baking soda
sultanas
brown sugar
icing sugar
violet water
oranges
lemons
rice
citron

currants
corn meal
apples
suet
lard
buttons
scissors
thread
needles
pins
Devil's Tongs *
English Lavender soap
cologne
tea
coffee
syrup
polish
fancy candles
stationery
notes
ribbons
dill
tumeric *

* See appendix.

My dear sister, Lucy Elizabeth, died today January 25, 1859, aged 28. She was frail from birth. She was very patient in her illness, loving; and, I always remember her knitting something useful for someone.

○———ᴄᴄᴄᴄᴠ⤳

"Our Chronicle"

May 1859

"The Spirit of the Times"

Vol. I   No. 4

Published by the
Members of Charlestown Lyceum

<u>U.R.S.</u>

<u>Terms:</u>

Free communication and good attention during the readings of its contents.

May this our paper e'er be filled
With gems of purest thought
May virtues' light be here distilled,
And wisdom's lesson taught.

<u>Today's Subject</u>

Mrs. H.B. Stowe's books on abolishing slavery.

Mrs. Sewall of Boston, lecturer.

○———ᴄᴄᴄᴄᴠ⤳

Salem 1825

From Java, Sumatra, and old Cathay,
Another ship is home today.
Now in the heat of the noon-day sun
They are unloading cinnamon.
And even here in Town House Square
The pungent fragrance fills the air;
Oh, nothing is quite so exciting to me
As a ship just home from the China Sea.
So I will go down to the harbor soon
And stand around all afternoon.

Are you in earnest? Siege this very minute.
What you can do, or dream you can, begin it.
Boldness has genius, power, and magic in it.
Only engage and then the mind grows heated.
Begin and then the work will be completed.

"Goethe"

I have decided that my favourite books are: "The Holy Bible,"
The Works of William Shakespeare, "Wuthering Heights,"
Emily Brontë, "Jane Eyre" Charlotte Brontë, all of Dickens'
works, "The Idylls of the King," Tennyson and all poetical
works. — Almost all.

I remember each spring how the Captain always made sure to present me with the first violets, lilies of the valley, and fragrant lilacs. But especially the first white Killarney rose that grew in his mother's garden. A cutting was brought from Ireland when the family came over to this country.

o———aaaaa⋌

"Lemon Cream Pie"

1 quart thick cream
1 well-beaten egg

Dusting of flour if the cream be not too thick. Sweeten and flavor with lemon. If the cream is very thick, the egg may be omitted. Fill a cooked pie shell and top with frothy sweetened cream.

o———aaaaa⋌

I know a bank where the wild thyme blows,
Where oxlips and the nodding violet grows;
Quite over-canopied with luscious woodbine,
With sweet musk-roses, and with eglantine:
There sleeps Titania sometime of the night,
Lulled in these flowers with dances and delight;
And there the snake throws her enamelled skin,
Weed wide enough to wrap a fairy in:
And with the juice of this I'll streak her eyes,
And make her full of hateful fantasies.

A Midsummer Night's Dream

o———aaaaa⋌

"Lemon Pie"

The Captain's Favourite

For crust: Take any biscuit cutter and cut from puff paste very thinly rolled, the bottom crust. Around the edge I curl a narrow strip of the paste and bake. While they are baking, I take my lemon and do not roll it but grate it — after the yellow rind is all grated I squeeze in the juice and a cup of sugar and the yolk of one egg. Stir well together. Upon this I pour a large cup of cold water (no milk) into which has been stirred a dessertspoonful of corn starch. Put all into a saucepan and stir until it is cooked into a rich, clear straw-coloured jelly. My crust being done, I fill them and take the white of the egg and beat. Put on the top and bake till just brown — about a minute — "very nice."

"The Captain's Comment"

"Common Mince Pies"

Cook a piece of lean, fresh beef until very tender. When cold, chop it very fine and take 3 times the quantity of apples, peeled and chopped fine and mix with the beef; add raisins, allspice; salt and sugar. Add molasses to suit the taste. A little ginger improves it. Small pieces of butter laid on top make it very tender.

"A Christmas Favourite"

57

"The Bugle Song"

Alfred, Lord Tennyson

The Splendour falls on castle walls
  And snowy summits old in story;
The long light shakes across the lakes,
  And the wild cataract leaps in glory.
Blow, bugle, blow, set the wild echoes flying,
Blow, bugle, answer, echoes, dying, dying, dying

"Corn Pone"

1 quart sweet milk
4 cups corn meal
2 cups of flour
½ teaspoonful salt
⅔ cup molasses or ½ will do
Mix and bake from 2½ to 3 hours.

How sweet the moonlight sleeps upon this bank!
Here will we sit, and let the sounds of music
Creep in our ears: soft stillness and the night
Become the touches of sweet harmony.

The Merchant of Venice

"Rice Pudding"

Ingredients:

One cupful of boiled rice (better if first cooked and still hot)
3 cupfuls of milk, 3/4 of a cupful of sugar, a tablespoonful of corn
starch; two eggs; add flavoring. Dissolve the corn starch first with
a little milk and then stir in the remainder of the milk, add the
yolks of the eggs and the sugar beaten together. Now put this over
the fire (there is less risk of burning in a custard kettle) and when
hot add the hot rice. Stir carefully until it begins to thicken like
boiled custard then take it off the fire and add the flavoring —
say extract of lemon. Put it into a pudding dish and place in oven.
Now beat the whites of the eggs to a stiff froth and add a little
sugar and flavoring. Take the pudding from the oven when colored
a little; spread the froth over the top and return to the oven for a
few moments to give the froth a delicate coloring.

I write to the Captain every day when he is away even though
he will receive my mail in great quantities as he reaches port. He
writes to me each day also and I treasure every single letter. He
says that life would be so lonely and meaningless if he did not have
my letters and special messages at holiday time to look forward to
and know that I am home at the end of each voyage, awaiting his
return.

"Ginger Cookies"

1 cup molasses, a piece of butter the size of an egg. Fill the cup with boiling water; 1 teaspoonful saleratus; 1 teaspoon ginger.

Flour to make thin. Chill dough. Roll out about ⅛ in. thick. Cut and bake about 8 minutes in medium oven. Makes delicious soft cookies.

"Schooner Cake"

Mary Sawtell's receipt

1 egg
1 cup sugar
1 cup milk
1 teaspoon cream tartar
½ teaspoon soda
½ cup shortening
2 cups of flour
Bake about 1 hour in a medium oven.

Come live with me and be my love,
And we will all the pleasures prove
That valley's groves, hills and fields,
Woods or steepy mountain yields.

Christopher Marlowe

Count your garden by the flowers
Never by the leaves that fall
Count your days by golden hours,
Don't remember clouds at all.
Count sights by stars, not shadows
Count your life by smiles not tears
And with joy on every morning
Count your age by friends not years.

———

"Blackberry Wine"

The blackberries must be full ripe and without blemish. Measure them. To every quart of fruit — allow a quart of clear, soft water. Boil the water by itself. Put the blackberries into a clean tub and mash them with a good spoon or mallet. When the water has boiled pour it on the blackberries and let it stand till next morning, in a cool place stirring it occasionally. Then press out all the juice. Measure it. To every quart of liquid allow half a pound of sugar. Put the sugar into a cask and strain the liquid upon it through a linen bag. Stir it frequently till the sugar is thoroughly dissolved. Let the cask remain unstopped till the liquid has done working. Then add half-ounce of isinglass* or an ounce of gum arabic* dissolved in a little hot water. You may substitute isinglass or gum arabic, the beaten whites of 4 eggs. Stir it often till next day. Then bung it. It may be bottled in 2 months. Currant wine can be made the same as above.

* See appendix.

"O Mistress Mine"

Wm. Shakespeare

O Mistress mine, where are you roaming?
O, stay and hear — your true love's coming,
That can sing both high and low.
Trip no further, pretty sweeting;
Journeys end in lovers' meeting,
Every wise man's son doth know.

"Cough Syrup"

Take thoroughwort*, horehound* and pennyroyal*. Take a good handful and boil them in just water enough to extract the strength. Then strain the liquid and add an equal quantity of molasses and boil until it forms a candy. Eat freely of this every time an inclination to cough is felt.

* See appendix.

"Care for Whooping Cough"

A teaspoonful castor oil to a teaspoonful of molasses, a teaspoonful of the mixture. To be given when the cough is troublesome and will afford relief at once, the same is good for croup if you have little children.

◦——〰〰〰〰〰✗

"The Rainbow"
The Book of Genesis

And God said — I do set my bow in the cloud, and it shall be for a token of a covenant between me and the earth. And it shall come to pass, when I bring a cloud over the earth, that the bow shall be seen in the cloud — While the earth remaineth, seed time and harvest, and cold and heat, and summer and winter, and day and night shall not cease.

◦——〰〰〰〰〰✗

Look upon the rainbow, and praise him that made it; very beautiful it is in the brightness thereof. It compasseth the heaven about with a glorious circle, and the hands of the most High have bended it.

"The Apocrypha"

◦——〰〰〰〰〰✗

"Beer"

4 pails of water
2 quarts of molasses
½ pounds of hops*
1 pint of barley

Add wintergreen to suit your taste and yeast enough to make it work.

o———⚊⚊⚊⟩⟩

"Yeast"

½ pint of hops
1 quart water
1 cup sugar
2 tablespoonsful of salt
1 spoonful of flour
½ pint of flour

Add dried yeast to rise. To be kept in bottles.

o———⚊⚊⚊⟩⟩

* See appendix.

"Washing Fluid No. 1"

sal soda — 1 lb.
stone lime — ½ lb.
waters — 5 quarts

Boil all a short time stirring occasionally. Then let it settle and pour off the clear fluid into a stone jug and cork for use. Soak your white clothes overnight in a simple water, wring out and soap wristbands, collars and have your boiler half-filled with water and when at scalding heat, put in one teacup of the fluid. Stir and put in your clothes and boil for half an hour. Then rub through one suds, rinsing in the blueing water and all is complete. For each additional boiler of clothes, add half a cup.

"Meat Pies"

1 pint dried apple, soak overnight, chop fine 2 cups raisins, chopped. ⅔ cup butter (½ will do) 1 teaspoonful of clove — also cinnamon; salt; 1 cup sugar; ⅔ cup molasses; 1 cup strong coffee; ½ cup vinegar. If the mixture is too thin, roll 2 crackers and add. If you have any bits of cold meat, chop and put in with rest of mixture. Sweeten to taste. You can use a larger quantity of apple if wanted.

If music be the food of love, play on —

Twelfth Night

"French Tea Biscuits"

Put yeast cake rising at night. In the morning take 3 cups milk; ½ cup yeast; ½ cup sugar and make a thin batter. At noon, thicken it with flour. That night knead and make into biscuits. Let it rise and bake for tea. Bake in moderate oven till light brown.

"Dainty and delicious."

"County Wexford Buns"

Mrs. Brigham's receipt

1 pint of milk
1 cup of sugar
1 cup yeast

Flour to make a batter; let it rise then add another cup of sugar; 1 cup butter; 1 egg and 1 nutmeg ground. Bake in a moderate oven for about 20 minutes or until golden color.

"Lines"

Lips I have kissed! will ye e'er fade away;
Hands I have pressed must ye ever decay.
Eyes that so warmly smiled upon me!
Will aught come to darken those glances I see;
O Death! cruel Death thou hast filled me with fear.
Wilt thou hide from my sight cherished and dear.
The form I have loved must it moulder away?
In the cold darkened tomb must my dearest ones lie?
Ah! yes cruel tyrant thou rulest us all.
We sooner or later must answer thy call
But turn now thy sickle away from our clime,
And stay not to sever. Now is not the time.
But Time speedeth fast we know not the hour,
And soon ah! full soon life must yield to Thy power
But the spirit — O Death thou canst not entomb.
Then let my sad heart no longer feel gloom.
I will cherish the soul! though the form may die.
My treasure will fade not nor vanish away!

B.V. Dickson

Lines written when I received word that my Captain and his ship had gone down during a terrible storm. After three soul-searing weeks of the most agonizing distress, 'though my faith was sorely tested and my heart so heavy, I could barely live through each day, his ship was sighted — listless and disabled but seaworthy and except for a touch of cold, my Captain was fine and arrived home within the month.

"Crossing the Bar"

Alfred, Lord Tennyson

Sunset and evening star
And one clear call for me!
And may there be no moaning of the bar,
   When I put out to sea.
For though from out our bourne of Time and Place
   The flood may bear me far,
I hope to see my Pilot face to face
   When I have crossed the bar.

"Rusk"

Mrs. Arthur Turner, West Riding, Yorkshire, England

1 pint of milk
1 coffee cup yeast
4 eggs

Flour enough to make it as thick as you can stir with a spoon. Let it rise very light but be sure it is not sour. If it is, work in half a teaspoon saleratus dissolved in a wine glass warm water. When this is light, work together 3/4 lb. of sugar and 9 ozs. of butter; add more flour if needed to make it stiff enough to mold. Let it rise again and when very light, mould it into small cakes. Bake 15 minutes in a quick oven and after taking it out, mix a little milk and sugar and brush over the rusk while hot with a small swab of linen tied to a stick and dry in the oven.

"For the Hair"

One pint of bay rum. Half an ounce of tincture of iron. An ounce of ammonia. Half-ounce essence of bergamot.* Three ounces Castile soap. One ounce table salt.

———

"Senna* Syrup"

Take senna, 3 ounces; boiling water, 1 pint; mix. Let it stand 24 hours. Then strain; add ½ lb. white sugar; scald and again strain and bottle and a tablespoonful pulverized cloves.

Dose: 2 or 3 tablespoonsful for the digestion.

———

"Washing Fluid No. 2"

5 ounces of lime
1 lb. sal soda
1 gal. boiling water

———

* See appendix.

"Orange Pies"

1 pint fresh, sweet milk
3 tablespoonsful flour
Boil them together then add:
   1 cup fine castor sugar
   1 sweet, juicy large orange
   the yolks of 2 eggs
   1 tablespoonful of butter then cool
   Place in a cooked pie shell.

Then take the whites of eggs and add 4 tablespoonsful of sugar. Make into frosting and bake brown in hot oven for a few minutes or until brown.

O, wonder! How many goodly creatures are there here! How beauteous mankind is! O brave new world that has such people in it.

"The Tempest"
Wm. Shakespeare

"Minute Pudding"

4 cups pounded crackers, 6 cups milk; boil it and stir in the crackers and boil 1 minute; add 2 even teaspoonsful salt; 2 eggs beaten and stirred in just before taken from the fire; very good without eggs. Eat with butter and sugar or sauce with a little vinegar boiled in.

"Floating Island"

Take 6 eggs; separate them; beat the yolks and stir into a quart of milk, sweeten to taste; flavor with nutmeg or lemon. Put this mixture into a pan, put some water in a saucepan and set it over the fire. When boiling put in your pan which ought to be half-immersed; keep stirring it until the custard gets thick. Beat the whites to a froth. When the custard is cold put it in a deep dish; heap the frothiest eggs upon it. Serve cold.

"Cup Cakes — Brigantines"

1 cup of butter
3 cups of loaf sugar*
4 large, fresh eggs
5 cups of flour
1 cup of fresh, new milk
1 cup cider
2 cups zante raisins
1 teaspoon soda
Bake in medium oven about 20–25 minutes.

* See appendix.

"Sponge Cake No. 1"

Miss Ida Turner — Loughborough, Lancashire, England

3 eggs
2 cups of flour
1 ½ cups of sugar
½ cup water
1 teaspoon cream of tartar
½ teaspoon soda
Bake in moderate oven about 1 hour.

"First Rate"

o——aaaao——x

"Mrs. Pierce's Tapioca Cream"

1 cup tapioca soaked overnight in water, put into a quart of cold milk in the morning. Let it cook slowly over steam until soft. Then take the yolks of 3 eggs & one whole one. Beat with 1 cup sugar & a little salt, stir into the milk, when boiling hot. Let it thicken but not boil. Beat the whites of the eggs with a spoonful of sugar & a little vanilla & heap on top of the cream & set in the oven to brown.

o——aaaao——x

I am knitting the Captain an oyster white Irish wool sweater. It is a special wool that fishermen wear. There's a natural oil in the wool to keep out the damp and keep in the comforting warmth.

o——aaaao——x

"Praise loudly, blame softly."

"Yorkshire Pudding"

Mrs. Mabel Burdine, Edinborough, Scotland

4 tablespoonsful flour
½ pint of sweet, fresh milk
1 tablespoonful water
2 eggs
a touch of salt

Put flour in bowl making a well in the middle. Mix in the milk, break in the eggs and beat well. Add this mixture to the flour, never the other way around. Leave the mixture to itself for about 1 hour. Mix in the water. Catch the drippings from the meat in a pan. Place in the oven till very hot and sizzling. Pour in mixture and bake in oven, a hot oven for 15 minutes. Then brown on top shelf for another five minutes. When pudding raises crisp and brown, it is ready to serve.

"Chocolate Candy"

1 cup of grated chocolate
1 cup milk
1 cup molasses
butter the size of an egg
1 cup of sugar

Boil an hour. Stir so it will not stick. Pour out in greased pan — add nuts and raisins if you wish.

○———◇

"Molasses Candy"

2 quarts of molasses
1 pound of brown sugar
juice of 2 large lemons
a teaspoonful essence of lemon
2 tablespoonsful of butter
peppermint flavoring

Stir constantly to a fast boil; add the butter — boil till a little of syrup dropped in cold water holds its shape. Remove and cool. When cool enough to handle add flavoring. Pull candy until it turns light in color and makes a rope 3/4 inches in diameter and cut in pieces.

○———◇

"Heart's Content"

"A sail, a sail! Oh, whence away,
And whither, o'er the foam?
Good brother mariners, we pray,
   God speed you safely home!"
"Now wish us not so foul a wind,
   Until the fair be spent;
For hearth and home we leave behind;
   We sail for Heart's Content."

"We sail for Heart's Content."

"For Heart's Content! And sail ye so,
   With canvas flowing free?
But, pray you tell us, if ye know,
   Where may that harbor be?
For we that greet you, worn of time,
   Wave-racked, and tempest-rent,
By sun and star, in every clime,
   Have searched for Heart's Content."

"Receipt for Cream Beer"

Maria E. Billings receipt

Take 2 oz. of tartaric acid, 2 lbs. of white sugar and the juice of half of a lemon and 3 pints of water, boil together 5 minutes; when nearly cold add the whites of 3 eggs, well-beaten with half a cup of flour and half an ounce of essence of checkerberry*. Bottle and keep in a cool place, and it is a very nice carbonate of soda.

○────ᴄᴏᴏᴏ🗡

"Verses for Autographs"

Fair book! thou art memory's treasure
To shine in the depth of the heart
A charm, to awaken new pleasure,
When others less cherished depart.
And love, truth and friendship forever
Shall sparkle the brightest for thee
Till death all these jewels dissever
And memory ceases to be.

If scribbling in albums will remembrance secure, with the greatest
of pleasure,
I'll scribble in yours.

When you're old and getting tea for your old man, remember me.

* See appendix.

Friendship commenced these lines
Memory holds them dear
And may you never forget the one
That wrote them here.

—o—∞∞∞—✗—

'Tis you I love and will forever,
You may change but I will never
But if you do these lines regret
Rub them out and me forget.
I've looked these pages o'er and o'er
To see what others wrote before and in this little lonely spot
I'll here inscribe "Forget me not!"

— — — — — Is the wish of your friend.

May thy lot be a happy one.

May thy course through life be ever onward and upward.

May thy bark sail smoothly o'er life's rough billow.
Is the heartfelt wish of your friend.

"Citron Cake"

5 cups of sugar
3 cups of butter
2 cups of sweet, fresh milk
10 cups of flour
6 eggs
1 glass of wine
1 glass of brandy
3 nutmegs, well-pounded
1 teaspoonful soda
1 pound of sultanas
¼ pound of citron
Bake about 1–1½ hours in a moderate oven.

"Sally Lunn"

Take about 2 cups flour; add 3 teaspoonsful baking powder; 1½ teaspoonsful salt. Cream ½ cup sugar with ⅓ cup butter; add to dry mixture. Bind with 1 cup milk and 2 eggs beaten up. Pour into small bake pan or pie pan and bake about 18–20 minutes in hot oven.

"Cornish Pasties"

Mrs. George Elliot

16 oz. stewing beef cut into small cubes; 16 oz. new white potatoes cut into small cubes; 1 large onion, diced; season with salt, fresh ground pepper, parsley, bay leaf.

Roll out short crust pastry 12" across. Put meat and vegetables on to pastry; add seasonings and 2 tablespoonsful beef broth. Damp edges and seal. Draw sealed edge to center and press into fluting. Brush pastry with beaten egg and bake for 15 minutes in hot oven then 1 hour in medium oven.

"Shopping"

October 2, 1859

I went to Boston today and purchased many things especially for my winter projects. It is a beautiful day, a typical "October day" in New England — blue skies, fluffy white clouds, golden sun, crisp air and trees whose leaves have turned every enchanting tint from gold to scarlet. I love New England any time of the year but the fall is my favourite time.

1. 1 pair red Morocco slippers — $5.00

2. 1 pair of black boots — $10.00

3. 1 pair of long, white kid gloves to wear at the opera — $5.00

4. 1 dozen pure, white, Irish linen handkerchiefs — edges to be tatted.

5. Material for a new quilt. I am going to make "The Rising Star Pattern."
    6 yds. red
    8 yds. white
    4 yds. blue

6. Wool knitting worsted for the Captain's blue quilt I am making for him to take on his next voyage.

7. Wool worsted to knit "Dutchess" 2 winter coats — one red — one blue; very patriotic.

8. Wool for emerald green shawl and one in heavenly blue.

9. Fringe for tablecloth.

10. Ecru thread to make fancy crochet cloth for teak wood diningroom table. Pick pattern.

11. Pick up new winter bonnet. Emerald green velvet, black ostrich plumes.
    Mrs. Nutting — $7.00

MRS. BONNETLOVE,
MILLINER.

PARISIAN STYLE: AMERICAN TASTE:
EXQUISITE CONTOUR.

"Sea Fever"
John Masefield

I must go down to the seas again, to the lonely sea and the sky,
And all I ask is a tall ship and a star to steer her by,
And the wheel's kick and the wind's song and the white sail's shaking,
And a gray mist on the sea's face, and a gray dawn breaking.
I must go down to the seas again, for the call of the running tide
Is a wild call and a clear call that may not be denied;
And all I ask is a windy day with the white clouds flying,
And the flung spray and the blown spume, and the sea gulls crying.
I must go down to the seas again, to the vagrant gypsy life,
To the gull's way and the whale's way where the wind's like a
    whetted knife;
And all I ask is a merry yarn from a laughing fellow-rover,
And quiet sleep and a sweet dream when the long trick's over.

"Lemon Custard"

1 lemon
1 cup of sugar
1 cup of milk
the yolks of three eggs
Cook, bring to boil — cool.
Place in pie shell and bake.

Take the whites of 3 eggs with sugar, beat to a froth. Put on the top and bake about 10–15 minutes in a hot oven.

81

"Sweet Pickles"

To 12 lbs. of cucumbers after the seeds are taken out and have been pared, boil in vinegar and water until soft. Then take out and have a syrup of 4 lbs. sugar and 1 quart vinegar and boil the fruit till boiled through.

❀

"Blanc Mange"
English

Mix in top of double boiler ½ cup sugar; 6 tablespoonsful cornstarch; ¼ teaspoonful salt. Gradually stir in 4 cups of milk. Place over boiling water 8–12 minutes until it thickens. Cover and cook 10 minutes more. Take one cup of mixture and stir into 2 well beaten eggs. Return to mixture and cook 2 minutes. When cool add 1 teaspoonful of vanilla and pour into a Turk's Head Mold.

❀

"The Lighthouse"
Sir Walter Scott

Far in the bosom of the deep,
O'er these wild shelves my watch I keep;
O ruddy gem of changeful light
Bound on the dusky brow of night,
The seaman bids my lustre hail,
And acorns to strike his timorous sail.

"Chocolate Creams"

Take half a cake of unsweetened chocolate grate and set over the tea kettle; while hot drop in the cream molds, which are made of two cups of sugar and half a cup of water; boil three minutes; after it begins to bubble remove from the stove and flavor with vanilla, stir until cold enough to make into molds; after the chocolate is added put them in buttered paper to harden.

"Tapioca Pudding"

Pare and core (with a tube) six or seven apples; lay them in a buttered dish. Pour over a cupful of tapioca or sago* one quart of boiling water, let it stand an hour; add two teacupsful of sugar; a little lemon; vanilla or wine. Pour this over the apples and bake an hour. Peaches (fresh or canned) may be substituted and are an improvement.

FLORAL EXHIBITION.

* See appendix.

"Christmas Season"

December 4, 1859

It's almost Christmas, our first together. Fortunately the Captain's voyage ended in August and he will not be leaving again until June, 1860.

I must start the plum puddings, 12th Night Cakes, fruit cakes, other special cakes, candies and mince meat. It is December 4th, St. Barbara's Day, my patron saint, and it is bitterly cold. The snow continues ceaselessly. The Captain spends many hours in the library studying his navigation charts and engineering formulae. I enjoy baking something special myself and bringing it into his study later in the evening. We sit close together before the roaring fire and share our deepest thoughts and feelings. I can hardly bear the thought of his leaving again in the spring.

"Whoever lives true life will love true love."

Elizabeth Barrett Browning

"This above all: to thine own self be true, And it must follow, as the night the day, Thou canst not then be false to any man,

"Hamlet"
Wm. Shakespeare

"December 26, 1859"

December 26 is St. Stephen's Day, my Captain's patron saint: We will exchange special gifts since it is also "Boxing Day." I have knitted him a nautical-blue coverlet for his bed aboard "The Golden Fleece."

"Old Irish"

The Wren, the Wren, the King of all Birds,
St. Stephen's Day was caught in the furze.
Although he's little, his family's great,
I pray you, good landlady, give us a trate.

"Third Anniversary"

March 18, 1860

Today was our third anniversary. It seems but yesterday when My Captain and I were married. We love each other even more this day, if possible. We celebrated with both his parents and my own. We all enjoyed one of the Captain's favourite dinners: Roast Beef, Yorkshire Pudding, Shrimp, Williamsburg Apple Pie, Prune Whip with a froth of cream and, of course, a special Cake — Chocolate throughout with silken icing. My parents presented us with a large antique Swiss-music box with inlaid mother of pearl that played many tunes. His parents gave us an Irish silver chocolate set, very old and very beautiful. I gave My Captain an embossed chiming watch and fob of purest gold engraved with this message, "Measure the time but never my love."

He presented me with the loveliest pin and matching ring of various precious stones. The pin forms a tree of life in gold encrusted with stones on every branch. Laid in succession, the first letter of each stone spells the word "Dearest." Diamond, emerald, amethyst, ruby, emerald, sapphire, and topaz.

To know that I am his "Dearest," not only in deed, but thought and word, as well, fills me with supreme joy and contentment. I am loved as only a woman should be loved. My Captain is loved as every man would want to be loved. Together we are truly one for all eternity.

My Captain leaves again in June for a journey to Canton. "Fair winds home, my darling."

"Outward Bound"

June, 1860

The most difficult part of waiting for my Captain is when he has just sailed to some strange seaport in a place that I know I shall never see. Once at sea, he is part of a world that I have no part of; I cannot share. My only rival for his constant and complete love and affection is "The Sea." When he gets that far-a-way look in his brilliant sea-blue eyes, I know that a new voyage is being planned. Then I wish with all my heart and soul that I could accompany him wherever he goes — just to be with him — to experience with him the powerful lure of the sea — that intoxicating feeling of freedom and adventure — the utter grandeur of it all. Anything so I do not have to stay home and wait and worry through the long endless months ahead. However, he will not permit it. The trips are swift, the seas treacherous, the dangers many and varied. He usually travels from Boston to the West Indies around the Horn to California, then the Sandwich Isles, Java, Sumatra, Ceylon and Canton exchanging cargoes at all these ports as he goes. This takes about three and one half months, then a weeks stay in Canton making repairs, loading up; then it's retrace the same route back to Boston for another three and one half months. He would have no peace of mind with me on board as he has so often said.

When I know he is homeward-bound, I like to spend as much time as possible in his library. I feel very close to him there. The beautiful walnut panelled walls complement the many models of famous ships displayed all around the room. His shell collection occupies an entire wall. Thousands of books on myriad subjects occupy the other walls. There is a large globe where I follow him as he sails around the world. I usually have a fire lit and sit at his beautiful hand-carved desk and write letters to him, do my house-hold accounts, keep up both my daily journal and receipt books. I do my needlework and practice my music at a small harpsichord I have brought in for practising.

Then later in the afternoon, I sit on the crimson velvet covered window seat in the large Bay window with my dogs and cats, enjoy my afternoon tea and watch the horizon intently in order to be sure to catch the first glimpse of the breath-taking sight of "The Golden Fleece" as she majestically enters the harbour. "My Captain has returned!"

"Election Cake No. 1"

Abraham Lincoln was elected Nov. 6, 1860.

1 pint bowl sugar
2 pints flour
½ pint butter
½ pint sour milk
1 pint raisins
1 pint currants
1 teaspoonful soda
1 teaspoonful cloves
1 teaspoonful nutmeg
6 eggs
½ cup Barbados molasses
Bake in moderate oven about 1–1½ hours.

"Election Cake No. 2"

4 lbs. flour
¾ lbs. butter
4 eggs
1½ lbs. sugar
1½ pt. good yeast
1 cup floured raisins

Wet with milk as soft as can be molded on a board. Set to rise.
Knead; add raisins. Set to rise again; put in greased pan and bake
45 minutes in a medium oven.

"Icing for Cake"

Take the white of one egg; a quarter of a pound of loaf sugar; a teaspoonful of gum dragon*. Melt and mix them into a paste and lay on the cake.

"New Year's"

Ring out, wild bells, to the wild sky,
　　The flying cloud, the frosty light:
　　The year is dying in the night;
Ring out, wild bells, and let him die.

Ring in the valiant man and free,
　　The larger heart, the kindlier hand;
　　Ring out the darkness of the land.
Ring in the Christ that is to be.

My dear brother Jonathan died December 6, 1860, aged 37. His ship went down in a terrible storm. His wife, my Captain's sister, Anna Maria died February 14, 1861 of consumption and a broken heart. She was only 37. Our two little nieces Carrie and Jennie Maria are left sadly orphaned. For the present, they will live with my brother Joseph and his wife Ann Dorothea who have a small daughter, Eva Maria. This I pray will help soften the terrible grief they are experiencing now at their great loss.

* See appendix.

Christmas "Marmion"
Sir Walter Scott

The damsel donned her kirtle sheen:
The hall was dressed with holly green;
Forth to the wood did merry-men go,
To gather in the mistletoe.
Then opened wide the baron's hall
To vassal, tenant, serf, and all —
Then came the merry maskers in,
And carols roared with blithesome din;
If unmelodious was the song,
It was a hearty note, and strong.
Who lists may in their mumming see
Traces of ancient mystery.

"Queen of Hearts Lemon Tarts"
Valentine's Day Favourite

The juice and grated rind of 2 lemons; 4 eggs; 2 cups white sugar; a piece of butter the size of an egg. Beat well together. Cook 1 hour over steam. This will make the filling for 50 tarts.

"Omelet"

Beat 2 eggs and stir one pounded cracker into them and fry in hot butter.

I have loved thee long, and I love thee now;
And, though the world should perish,
Over its dying embers still would glow
The flames of the love I cherish.

Heinrich Heine

"Nice Pudding"

Into one pint of flour stir two teaspoonful of baking powder and a little salt using milk to make a soft batter. Place five buttered cups in a steamer, drop a large spoonful of batter in each cup, then a layer of berries or tart apples (chopped) or jelly then fill the cups ¾ full of the batter. Steam 20 minutes. Use any sweet sauce or cream and sugar.

"Tomorrow is St. Valentine's Day, all in the morning betime,
And I a maid at your window, To be your Valentine."

Hamlet, Act IV
Wm. Shakespeare

"Hot Cabinet Pudding"

Mrs. Philos Stewart

Spatter butter in a baking pan and fill it with layers of stale cake cut up in pieces, sprinkle chopped figs, dates or prunes. Mix together 2 cups milk, 2 large beaten eggs, ½ cup sugar, 1 teaspoonful vanilla. Pour over cake and fruit. Bake in a medium oven about 35–40 minutes. Serve hot whipped sweetened cream.

"Irish Plum Cake"

1 lb. flour; ½ lb. butter; ½ lb. sugar; ¾ lb. currants; ¾ lb. sultanas; 2 oz. mixed peel; 2 oz. ground sweet almonds; 1 oz. ground bitter almonds; 2 oz. treacle*; dissolve soda in 1 tablespoonful of hot water, add to liquid and mix cake thoroughly. Bake in 2 small, or one large tin, in moderate oven for 2–3 hours. Keeps well and is lovely iced with almond icing, and butter or water icing on top.

The Captain's mother always serves this cake decorated with shamrocks on St. Patrick's Day to honor the beloved saint and to keep this lovely tradition alive.

ERIN GO BRAGH

* See appendix.

"Old Irish"

"Wilt Thou steer my frail black bark
O'er the dark, broad ocean's foam?
Wilt Thou come, Lord, to my boat
Where afloat, my will would roam?
Thine the mighty, Thine the small,
Thine to make men fall like rain,
God, wilt Thou grant aid to me
As I come o'er the upheaving main?"

"The man who fights for his ideals is the man who is alive."

"Don Quixote"
Cervantes

Some new vocal music arrived today from London. I can barely wait to learn them. They are so unusual and melodious. Handel, Bach, Purcell, Mozart, Bellini, Verdi, Donizetti, Ballads from Ireland, England, Scotland, Wales, Hebrides and so much more!

"Union Cake"

Receipt from General Halbrook's wife, Matilda 1862

1 cup butter
2 cups sugar
½ cup corn starch
3 cups flour
1 cup milk
4 eggs
1 teaspoonful tartar
½ teaspoonful soda
and use mace
Bake about 1 hour in a medium oven.

Stanza

Emily Brontë

Often rebuked, yet always back
    To those first feelings returning that were born with me.
And leaving busy chase of wealth and learning
    For idle dreams of things which cannot be.
I'll walk when my own nature would be leading:
    It vexes me to choose another guide:
Where the grey flocks in ferny glens are feeding,
    Where the wild wind blows on the mountain side.

"Loaf Cake"

Wartime 1863

 2 cups flour

2 eggs

1 teaspoonful mace

1/8 teaspoonful salt

1 teaspoonfull lemon rind, grated

1 teaspoonful cream of tartar

½ teaspoonful soda

1 cup molasses

½ cup butter — creamed

1 cup currants

1 cup sultanas

Mix, pour in greased loaf pan and bake in medium oven for about one hour.

Hie Away!
Sir Walter Scott

Hie away, hie away!
Over bank and over brae,
Where the copsewood is the greenest,
Where the fountains glisten sheenest
Where the lady fern grows strongest
Where the morning die lies longest
Where the black cock sweetest sips it,
Where the fairy lastest trips it;
Hie to haunts right seldom seen,
Lovely, lonesome cool and green,
Over bank and over brae,
Hie away, hie away!

"The Rescue"

May 1863

During the Civil War, my Captain delivered military supplies and food for our brave soldiers down along the coast to Southern Ports. On one journey homeward he became involved in a harrowing rescue at sea.

Upon arriving at his destination, he discovered that the prevailing weather conditions were so favorable that they were able to sail directly to their anchorage without the aid of a tug or pilot boat. But now, as they prepared to return to the home port of Boston this early morning they found that the wind was rising steadily. The Captain was on the quarter deck with the harbour pilot who had been taken aboard in order to guide them out as far as the open water because of the thrashing seas. The Captain issued commands to the First Mate. "Prepare to cast off, Mr. Farrell."

"Aye, Aye, sir," was the quick reply.

All work being done to the accompaniment of varied full-throated sea shanties, the anchor was hove up and away. The wind was steadily increasing and there was already a good deal of restless swell to the sea. The sails were then unfurled. Suddenly, the Captain spied a little black girl about eleven running toward the ship with two men in pursuit — probably slave bounty hunters. She was clutching her cloak tightly about her pathetically thin little body. The Captain quickly ordered a line over the side and up she hastily scrambled much to the anger and dismay of the hunters. Anxious hands pulled her safely over the side. The line was immediately hauled in and the signal given. "Get underway at once, Mr. Farrell." The great ship moved majestically out to sea guided by the harbour Pilot who then dropped down a line to his boat and returned to the dock. The ensign halyards were then raised; the Stars and Stripes billowed back from the stern; the helmsman grasped the wheel, shaped her course and held her steady as she goes. The taut, wind-filled sails strained the ropes. The hoisted sheets swelled and caught the mighty winds with a sharp crackling, ear-splitting sound that reverberated over the restless fomenting waters. They continued to fill as into the roaring sea the clipper ship glided, gathering speed faster and faster, heading straight for the open seas and home. The ship was now on its own; the waters rushed backward from the sharp bow to rush aft in a great froth and mingle with the foaming white wake beyond the stern.

As soon as they were safely on the high seas, the Captain ordered the little girl brought to his quarters. She, who had been so brave before was now trembling with fear as the tall, stern-looking Captain began to question her. "What is your name and where are you from, little lady?" asked the Captain.

She replied, "My name is Mariah. I lived on a plantation in Virginia. After it was burned to the ground, my mammy and I ran away. She was taken sick and died about two months ago. Before she died she told me to run to the North, head toward the sea. Maybe someone would take me aboard a ship. I traveled by nite and hid by day, living on anything I could find. I was scared and missed my Mammy so, but I kept hearing her say: "Child, go North and find freedom somehow." I kept running until I was within sight of the dock and your ship. Then those two hunter men saw me and give chase. I prayed so hard and you saw me and here I be."

The Captain ordered hot blankets and food for her immediately.

As he helped her to remove her tattered cloak, he heard a baby wail and with great disbelief carefully lifted a little two-month old baby from a sack attached to her back. She told how her Mammy died when brother Isaiah was born. Then a pathetic meow was heard as a tiny half-starved tabby cat poked its head from another sack tied to her bodice. The Captain threw back his head and laughed. "Wait 'til my Lady sees what treasures I am bringing to her on this voyage. A little girl to be companion to my nieces Carrie and Jennie Maria, an official mouse-catcher for Rosewood and another little baby orphan to raise. All in all a handsome bounty for my Lady's pleasure. We're homeward bound and clear of danger so let's crowd those sails Mr. Farrell. I have a Lady waiting in Boston for this precious cargo!"

> "But now our trip is over and we don't have a care,
>   We'll bend on all our stu'n sails and sail for Yankee Land, singing,
> Blow, ye winds in the morning,
>   blow, ye winds, heigho
> Clear away your running gear and
>   blow, ye winds, heigho."

Today my dear brother Charles' dog, King, died. He was never quite the same after my brother's death. We buried him in a special place in the garden we reserved as a memorial for those members of the family who never returned from the seas. The flag is always kept flying and there is a small gazebo where we can sit and remember. We always feel as if the spirits of our loved ones are very close.

"O God, take Thy small servants, those furred and feathered creatures of myriad kinds to Thy Celestial home. Take them, who have brought unswerving devotion and comfort to Thy human folk and oh! let them lie before the hearths of heaven in sweet repose until they and we meet again to roam the byways of Paradise together for all eternity."

Praise God the terrible War is over. General Robert E. Lee of the South surrendered to our General Ulysses S. Grant today April 9, 1865 at Appomattox, Virginia.

Abraham Lincoln died today April 15, 1865. May our Heavenly Father in His Great Mercy preserve the Union and sustain Mrs. Lincoln in this darkest of hours.

"Shopping for Summer"

June 1, 1865

Today my mother and I went to Boston town to select summer wardrobes. Mother selected frocks, gowns for evening, etc., in mauves, violets and lilac. With her pretty gray hair, they are most becoming. I needed all sorts of outfits. They are as follows:

1. Pink muslin trimmed with white eyelet flounced underskirts, broad sash and puffed sleeves.
2. White cashmere over acqua-blue silk petticoats, low round neck, trimmed with heavy fringe.
3. Three linen dresses, very smart, worn over flounced underskirts and many blue silk petticoats, one embroidered in white, one in red and one in green. The dresses are red, white and green respectively.
4. A black braided jacket and skirt with matching straw hat covered with green and white flowers.
5. A beautiful leghorn hat, the crown covered with pink damask roses and leaf green velvet streamers to tie around my chin.
6. Parosols of cane, white silk, French blue, jade green and pink, all trimmed in wide ruffles.
7. A lovely blue faille silk right from Paris, trimmed in pink silk flowers. A very low neck; "I feel so daring."
8. Three walking dresses: One navy over a cerise taffeta petticoat; one brown over a French blue petticoat and one black over an emerald green petticoat.
9. A white dainty muslin trimmed with valenciennes lace over pink silk. This I shall take home with me. Miscellaneous

bonnets, hats, gloves, reticules, etc.

Then we had a lovely lunch at my Aunts; visited for a while and made one more stop at the Apothecary before returning home. An apothecary shop is indeed a fascinating place. The scents are tantalizing, the strange names so intriging and the goods themselves so interesting. We bought many bars of Grossmith's white rose and cucumber soap and lotions of Cucumber to preserve the Complexion. Then, of course, glycerine and rosewater lotion, swansdown puffs, sponges, almond meal, witch hazel, nail brush and buffer, tooth brushes, dentifrices and white rose fragrance in the prettiest container.

June 3 is the Captain's birthday and I have a large party planned just for our families. I shall wear the white muslin over the pink silk in his honour.

I bought some very special candies as an extra gift for My Captain.

A very tiring day but also very rewarding!

My sister-in-law, Elsbeth Maeve, died today June 19, 1866. She would have made a great Sea Captain. She was a woman far ahead of her time. She possessed a great scientific and mathematical mind. She was my Captain's favourite sister and he took great pride in her intellect.

"Prune Apricot Pie"

1 lb. dried prunes
½ lb. dried apricots

Soak — drain and keep juice. Add ¼ tsp. nutmeg; ¼ tsp. cinnamon to ¾ cup of fruit juice; 1 tablespoonful cornstarch; ½ cup white sugar; 2 tablespoonsful lemon juice and 1 tablespoonful butter. Bring to a boil. Roll out crust, line large pie plate. Place fruit neatly and cover with liquid. Make lattice work top crust and spatter with butter. Bake in medium oven about 35–40 minutes. Serve with sweetened frothy cream.

"Delicious"

July 15.

St. Swithin's Day, if thou dost rain,
For forty days it will remain;
St. Swithin's Day, if thou be fair.
For forty days 'twill rain nae mair.

"Lancashire Fruit Cake"

2 cups fresh butter
3 cups fine white sugar
5 cups of flour
1 cup of fresh, sweet milk
2 cups of currants
4 large fresh eggs
1 teaspoonful cloves, cinnamon and nutmeg
Bake in a medium oven about 1 hour.

"O For a Booke"
Old English

O for a Booke and a shadie nooke,
    eyther in-a-doore or out;
With the grene leaves whispering overhede,
    or the Streete cryes all about.
Where I maie Reade all at my ease,
    both of the Newe and Olde;
For a jollie goode Booke whereon tok looke
    is better to me than Golde.

104

"23rd Psalm"

The Lord is my shepherd; I shall not want. He maketh me to lie down in green pastures: he leadeth me beside the still waters. He restoreth my soul: he leadeth me in the paths of righteousness for his name's sake. Yea, though I walk through the valley of the shadow of death I will fear no evil: for thou art with me; thy rod and thy staff they comfort me. Thou preparest a table before me in the presence of mine enemies: thou anointest my head with oil; my cup runneth over. Surely goodness and mercy shall follow me all the days of my life: and I will dwell in the house of the Lord forever.

The Captain brought me a small, white, curly-haired terrier when he returned from his Liverpool voyage. She is to be called the "Dutchess of Skye" because she comes from the "Isle of Skye." She has big, bright, black eyes, has a really sweet smile and lifts her little paw so daintily. She is so obedient already. She is a great comfort and joy to me while the Captain is at sea. She seems to enjoy sitting on her little velvet cushion as I play the Melodeon and practise my singing. She also likes it when I play the large, grand piano.

September 1867

"Mrs. Bacheldor's Lemon Pie"

1 cup fine castor sugar
yolks of 2 eggs, large and fresh
2 tablespoonsful cornstarch
the juice and rind of 1 lemon
1 cup hot water

Pour on the whole and come to a boil. Bake the crust, cool and pour cool custard in it. Then beat the whites of the eggs; add sugar. Cover the top of the pie and bake until light brown.

When the Captain came home from his last voyage, he brought me the loveliest hand-carved scrimshaw pendant, earrings, ring and bracelet with various pictures on them, the Clipper, our home, "Rosewood", my little Dutchess and Killarney roses. Mr. Farrell, the Captain's first mate carved them for me.

* See appendix.

The Captain's mother came to spend a fortnight with us before he sails to the West Indies. her husband had to go south on a business trip. She is such a lovely, intelligent lady, very particular in everything she does. However, she seems to find my pursuits to her liking. We think alike on so many things, books, poems, music, politics, clothes, flowers, food — housekeeping in general. We share a very deep love of the classics — music, art and literature — also joy and laughter, the study of the moon, the sun, the stars, the universe, the heavens — but most of all we share the same esteem for the Captain. Her beloved son and my very dear and cherished husband.

I am so thankful that she lives only across the river.

This will be the Captain's last voyage. He is retiring this coming year in June 1871. He is joining the family mercantile establishment and will be home at last to stay. I am so very happy.

"Mock Pie"

1 cup of dried apple chopped partly fine and some in large strips. Pile into a tin pan with a little water; then add 2 cups of molasses. Let is boil a long time until the apple is all saturated.

Now add 1 egg; a teaspoonful of cloves; 1 teaspoonful of cinnamon; ½ teaspoonful of nutmeg; 1 teaspoonful soda with flour; a little salt; 1 teacupful of shortening of most anything you like or have convenient.

○────⋙─⨞

I am very sad today. I received word that the Captain's ship will be delayed a month because of the inclement weather over the Atlantic. They were blown 1,000 miles off their course and will have to tack all the way back home.

May 3, 1871

"Mystic Molasses Cookies"

His mother's own receipt.
The Captain's favourite cookie.

1 egg
1 cup sugar
1 cup molasses
½ cup lard or butter
teaspoonful of saleratus
⅓ cup of water

Mix soft and bake on greased cookie sheet for 8–10 minutes in a medium oven or until done.

"Summer Shopping List"

Boston, June, 1871

1. Summer calico prints and plain for dresses, morning gowns.
   40 yards @ .12½ $5.00

2. Blue denim
   Gingham
   Delaine
   Lonsdale cambric
   Irish lace trim

3. 1 New summer bonnet of pink silk cabbage roses and taffeta ribbands.

   1 Large Leghorn straw trimmed with pink roses and velvet ribbands to be worn with a rose cotton embroidered lace gown. I will wear this at my niece, Lucy Phillips' wedding.

4. 24 yds. fine chambray for 6 new summer shirts for the Captain.

5. Order an entire new non-nautical wardrobe for the Captain.

"They That Go Down"

Psalm 107:23–33

They that go down to the sea in ships, that do business in great waters;
    these see the works of the Lord, and his wonders in the deep.
For he commandeth and raiseth the stormy wind
    which lifteth up the waves thereof.
They mount up to the heaven, they go down again to the depths:
    their soul is melted because of trouble.
They reel to and fro, and stagger like a drunken man,
    and are at their wits' end.
Then they cry unto the Lord in their trouble,
    and he bringeth them out of their distresses.
He maketh the storm a calm
    so that the waves thereof are still,
Then are they glad because they be quiet;
    so he bringeth them unto their desired haven.
Oh that men would praise the Lord for His goodness,
    and for His wonderful works to the children of men!

"Breakfast Cakes — Muffins"

1 pint milk
1 tablespoon melted butter
1 tablespoon molasses
1 egg
1 tablespoon yeast

Stir it up overnight. In the morning put in a teaspoonful soda dissolved in a little water. Flour enough to make a thick batter. Bake about 20–25 minutes in a hot oven.

"Sweet Pickled Tomatoes"

1 peck tomatoes; 6 onions sliced; 1 cup salt; let stand overnight, drain off the water. Boil 20 minutes; drain through a sieve; 2 teaspoonsful each: allspice; cinnamon; cloves, mustard seeds; black pepper; 1 lbs. sugar; 3 quarts vinegar; 1 quart water and simmer slow.

"Tomatoe Catsup"

Take a gallon of skinned tomatoes.
4 tablespoonsful salt
4 tablespoonsful black pepper
3 of mustard

Grind these articles fine and simmer them slowly in sharp vinegar, 3 or 4 hours and then strain it through a sieve and bottle, close. Use enough vinegar to make half a gallon of liquor when the process is over.

"Pickles"

Drop the cucumbers into boiling water but not boil them. Let them remain ten minutes, wipe them dry. Drop them into cold spiced vinegar. This brine will not keep long in warm weather but in cold it is first rate.

"Pickled Tomatoes"

1 peck of tomatoes, chopped fine
2 quarts vinegar
½ cup cloves
½ cup white mustard
1 cup whole allspice
2 cups sugar
½ cup pepper
6 green peppers chopped
Mix all together and stir until done.

"Pickled Peaches"

Rub off the wooley stuff and do not pare them. Put three cloves into each peach; put one quart molasses to 3 quarts vinegar on the stove to boil and then pour it on the peaches while hot for three mornings and then it is ready for use the rest of the year.

"The Death of My Uncle Stephen Phillips"

July 8, 1871

My dear uncle Stephen Phillips died today. He was born November 11, 1791. It is a very sad time for our family because he was my dear father's only living kin. My aunt Victoria is grief-stricken. Theirs was a long and abiding marriage filled with much happiness. Rosalind, their only child, died the year I was born and they often said I was like another daughter to them. My parents allowed me to spend summers with them at their magnificent estate: Rosemeathe. Whenever I visited there, my uncle would take time to teach me the intricacies of higher mathematics, navigation and astronomy; then, together we would go for rides through the grounds of the estate. My Welsh pony, Princess, was given to me one birthday. I loved her and took care of her myself. My uncle and I would play croquet, tennis and badminton.

My uncle was a retired sea-Captain and delighted in telling me tales of the sea monsters sighted off of Gloucester; and thrilling stories of how he outdistanced Chinese pirates while on the China Seas. He also taught me many of the sea songs (manavilins) and sea shanties (work songs). The former were sung by the sailors for fun and the latter only for work. My favourite shantie has always been "Rolling Home" a haunting melody that my uncle would sing for me. Other evenings we would play backgammon, chess or checkers.

I loved him like a second father and he loved me like a dear daughter. I do so wish my Captain were here with me at this sad time.

> "Naught from death can fly
> No friend but what must part
> Death will dissolve the tend'rest tie
> That's formed within the heart."

"Apple Brown Betty"

Mrs. Francis

Melt ¼ cup butter with 1 ⅓ cups bread crumbs, add 4–5 cups tart apples — cut up; 1 cup brown Barbados sugar; 1 teaspoonful cinnamon; ¼ teaspoonful salt. Place part of bread in the bottom of greased baking pan; add layers of apple with bread cubes; end with bread. Pour 2 tablespoonsful lemon juice o'er all plus ⅓ cup water. Bake in medium oven for 1 hour.

You can also dribble ½ cup melted butter over all before baking.

"Chocolate Eclairs"

1 cup of hot water; ½ cup of butter, boil together, stirring in a cupful of dry flour while boiling. When cold, add 3 eggs not beaten. Drop by tablespoonsful on a buttered tin, and bake in a quick oven 25 min.; be careful not to open the oven door more than is absolutely necessary. This makes 15 puffs.

For the Cream: 1 cup of milk; ½ cup of sugar; 1 egg and 3 tablespoonsful of flour. Boil as for any custard, flavor with vanilla. When both this and the puffs are cool, open and fill.

"Honey"

Put 1 pint of water (in cold weather use a little more and at anytime it is safer to use more rather than less) and a piece of alum* one fourth as large as a medium-sized nutmeg into any nicely-cleaned kettle over a bright fire and bring to a brisk boil; set the kettle off and into the solution therein. Put 4 pounds of white sugar; stir together, place over the fire and bring to a sharp, brisk, boiling for one or two minutes; remove from the fire, and strain through a light cotton cloth.

o—⁓⁓⁓ᴈ

"Spider Cake"

Take your 12" black spider and splatter well with butter; mix together:

> 1/3 cup regular flour
> 1 2/3 cups Indian meal*
> 1 cup of fresh, sweet milk
> 1/2 cup Barbados sugar or molasses
> 1 teaspoonful salt
> 3 eggs, beaten
> 1 tablespoonful lard or oil

Beat everything very well. Pour batter into pan and put into a medium-hot oven. After a while, pour a cup of sweet milk on top and don't mix. It makes like a custard. Bake for 1/2 hour.

o—⁓⁓⁓ᴈ

* See appendix.

"The Death of My Aunt
Victoria Mary Phillips"

August 1, 1871

My dear Aunt Victoria died today, August 1, exactly 24 days
after my dear uncle. She was so close to him in life that I know
she would only want to be close to him in death.

She was born in Scotland, November 17, 1797 in a grand
estate next to Glamis Castle. In those days, being an only
daughter, she was permitted to study singing and pianoforte.
Through the years she attained a high degree of proficiency at both
arts and was noted for her exquisite oratorio and opera singing.
When my Uncle Stephen was on a voyage to the British Isles, he
met her, immediately became fascinated with her, proposed, was
accepted and married in a very short time; one month to be exact.
They sailed for Boston where my uncle built for her the magnificent
Georgian estate called "Rosemeathe" which he filled with countless
rare and beautiful furnishings from China and other places. I was
very fortunate because she taught me how to sing and play the
piano. Many an evening we would gather in the music room and
after enjoying a high tea before the blazing hearth, I would entertain
with songs by Francis Hopkinson, namely: "My days have been
so wondrous free," "Enraptured I Gaze," and "My Love is Gone
To Sea," while my aunt played the harpsichord and my uncle,
the Dulcimer.

She possessed that peculiar combination of spirit and brains that
lights a personality with charm. She would let me play with curious

things my uncle had brought back from China — especially a hand-carved ivory chess set. On my thirteenth birthday, she brought me to hear "The Swedish Nitengale," Jenny Lind, at the Temple in Boston town and also gave me a pale blue leather Journal — silver bound with lock and key to record my life.

She taught me how to knit coverlets, blankets, and many lovely things for my hope chest.

I shall miss her very much.

Aunt Victoria

"Here died and here
        with her forefathers sleep
the admirable and beauteous
        Victoria Mary Haworth Phillips
Consort of Stephen Phillips."

"Baked Eggs"

Mrs. Devon

Take a deep pie plate and put into it a piece of butter the size of an egg; set it in the oven to dissolve and when melted, break in carefully eggs enough to cover the bottom of the plate; return to the oven until the white is firm and you will have a very handsome as well as an edible dish. Salt and pepper to taste.

"Boiled Rice"

2 cups rice
6 cups cold water

Wash the rice and put in a tin. Boil with a tight cover and sit in a boiler of hot water; cover it tightly. It will need no stirring; add seven spoonsful of salt. Boil 1½ hours.

"Ham Loaf"

Take 2 pounds of lean smoked ham and grind with 2 pounds of fresh ground pork; add 2 chopped onions; 3 eggs; 1½ cups bread crumbs and 1½ cups milk. Put mixture in large loaf pan and bake in a slow oven for 2 hours.

"Raisin Sauce"

1 ⅓ cups water
1 cup plump sultanas
2 tablespoonful vinegar
2 tablespoonful fresh lemon
1 teaspoonful dry mustard
⅔ cup Barbados brown sugar

Cook everything together; when boiling, add cornstarch dissolved in water. Cook until clear.

"Beef Stew and Dumplings"

Mrs. Francis

Place about 2 lbs. of fresh beef cut up in 2" pieces, roll in flour, salt and pepper until covered. Brown in large, black iron kettle. Use dripping or sal tpork for browning. Add 8 carrots, 5 medium onions and 10 medium-sized potatoes. Cover with water and cook all until tender. Add thyme, parsley and bay leaf. When all is cooked and tender add a little flour and water rubbed together smoothly with ½ cup melted butter. Make common dumplings and drop on gently bubbling stew.

"Soft Gingerbread"

"Nice"

4 teacups flour

2 cups molasses

½ cup butter

2 cups buttermilk or sour milk

1 cup of thick cream

3 eggs

1 tablespoonful of ginger and the same of saleratus

Mix them all together with the exception of the buttermilk in which the saleratus must be dissolved and then added to the rest. Bake in a medium oven about 40 minutes.

"To Sugar Pop Corn"

Put into an iron kettle one tablespoonful butter, 3 of water and one teacup white sugar, boil until ready to candy then throw in 3 quarts corn nicely popped, stir briskly until the candy is evenly distributed over the corn. Set the kettle from the fire and stir until it is cooled a little and you have each grain separate and crystalized with sugar. Care should be taken not to have too hot a fire lest you scorch it any. Nuts of any kind prepared in this way are delicious.

"Rice Pudding"

Mrs. Abner Cook

4 tablespoonful of rice — soaked overnight
4 tablespoonful of sugar
1 quart sweet milk
a little salt

Bake 2½ hours in a moderate oven set in another container of water.

"Gingerbread"

2 teacupsful flour, ½ cup soft Barbados sugar, 1 teaspoonful ginger, 1 teaspoonful cinnamon, pinch salt, 1 teaspoonful baking soda, 1 tablespoonful molasses, ½ cup milk, 2 oz. lard, 1 tablespoonful syrup, 1 teaspoonful mixed spice, 2 eggs, ½ lb. sultanas, floured.

Well-greased baking tin. Dissolve baking soda in a little milk, melt syrup, molasses and lard in pan, sieve dry ingredients and mix well. Make hole in center and pour the melted mixture in along with eggs and milk and baking soda. Mix all together. Pour into grased tin and bake for 40 min. in moderate oven.

"The Legacy of Love"

September 3, 1871

Yesterday I was informed by my Aunt's lawyer that I was to be the sole heir to her estate. I still can hardly believe it. She left this letter to me:

August 2, 1871

Dearest niece,

Since your birth you have brought great joy not only to your family but to your uncle and myself as well. You have shared so much of your love of life and joy in living with us that we deem it only fit and proper that you should be our only heir. We wish you to be Mistress of Rosemeathe and your Captain, a fitting Master. All monies and things of value are to be yours so that you will be an independent woman as I was. Your uncle especially desired this. Together we leave you this legacy of love.

With much love, my dear,
your devoted,
Aunt Victoria

Today is the first day that I have been back to Rosemeathe since my Aunt's death. It is such a magnificent estate, twice as large as Rosewood, with vast lands, stables, and gardens. It is a very large establishment with many servants. I feel very strange and a bit lonely walking through the echoing chambers. They contain so many beautiful treasures from my Uncle's voyages around the world: hand-painted wallpaper depicting Chinese scenes, hand-carved mantlepieces, Porcelain jardiniere, sets of Irish Beleek, English Wedgewood, silverware of all descriptions and furniture in all styles and periods. I opened the hidden safe and removed velvet cases containing matchless jewels of inestimable value. Opals, diamonds, star sapphires and my favourites — emeralds. I replaced the sparkling jewels and continued my walk through the house, rediscovering old nooks and crannies I loved so well as a child. I then proceeded up the narrow stairs into the attic and then climbed up the last pair of stairs to the roof and the "Widow's Walk" that extended the length of the house from chimney to chimney. The day was overcast with a promise of rain and fog. A hint of autumn chill roused me from my reverie of things and times past and brought me downstairs again, down to the special place that my Aunt gave me for my very own. I quickly walked to the Gallery; a long, lofty suite of rooms panelled in English walnut taken from an old ship. There were high-backed chairs, tables, firescreens, dressers — all the furniture brought to Rosemeathe from her ancestral home in Scotland. This place she called her family remembrance apartment. I quickly walked to a wall covered by a heavy tapestry, briefly glanced at the tall suit of armour standing guard and pulled the curtain back. On the wall revealed was embossed a shield which I pressed and a door slowly opened. I lit a taper that I was carrying and started up the staircase to another room. Now, I was in my own special place. There my girlhood treasures were assembled; Dolls, trunks of dress costumes from my aunt's cast-off gowns, books, puzzles, dried up paints with stiffened brushes, toys of all description — the mementos of a very happy childhood. I sat down at my pretty little table and wept for my aunt and uncle and all the happy times we had shared together.

My Captain will arrive three months later than expected; early October instead of late June. Then we will move into Rosemeathe and probably let Rosewood out to someone in the family. I know I shall love and care for this great place and with my Captain's help we will enjoy it just the way my Aunt and Uncle intended we should.

"Sago Pudding"

Mrs. Brigham's receipt

1 quart milk
6 spoonsful sago
6 spoonsful sugar
2 eggs
salt, spices
Bake an hour.

"Tapioca Cream"

Soak 2 spoonsful tapioca for several hours.
Boil 1 quart milk, add the yolks of 3 eggs well-beaten with ½ cup sugar. Add 1 teaspoon vanilla and set away to cool.

126

"Snow Pudding"

2 tablespoonsful of tapioca soaked overnight in enough water to cover it. Add 1 quart of milk that has been allowed to boil.

3 eggs
1 cup sugar

Beat the yolks of the eggs and sugar and tapioca together and stir. Take the boiling milk; let it boil till it thickens. Beat the whites to a stiff froth and put them into the pudding dish and pour the hot pudding over it. Bake about 1 hour in a moderate oven.

"Orange Soufflé"

Peel the oranges, take out the seeds and cut them in small pieces in the dish you wish to serve it in. Sprinkle with sugar quite thick, then make a nice boiled custard of the yolks of the eggs leaving out as many whites as would make a nice covering for the top, pour it over the oranges when cold — not filling the dish quite full. Beat the whites to a stiff froth and pile on the top (put sugar in the white) then set the dish in a dish of cold water and place the whole in the oven. Let it brown lightly.

"My Captain"

My Captain is a man of character, intellect, courage, honor strength; moral as well as physical. A man of daring, adventure, vision, he has his eye fixed on the North Star with his hand at the helm and is able to chart and hold a true course. He is skilled in the ways of the sea and possesses all the necessary instincts of a deep water sailor, especially the ability to feel his way through shrouds of fog and darkness and bring his ship into safe harbour. His great compassion enables him to handle relationships with people of all characters and nationalities. The determination, dedication and devotion he expends on his many enterprises are noteworthy. Besides being an astute businessman, he is also an engineer, astronomer and navigator. His deep love of nature is revealed in his descriptions of sunsets in the South Seas, sea gulls flying overhead, then darting into the opalescent waters which are fairly leaping with silvery fish.

Aboard ship his life is filled with loneliness, because to maintain order he must isolate himself from his crew. A steward attends to his needs and serves him his meals alone for he must eat in seclusion. The technicalities of charts and maps occupy many hours of his time and the successful completion of the long voyage depends on his astuteness in these areas. His moments of relaxation are spent in the study and collecting of shells, buying unusual objects of art for our home and smoking his pipe. He takes great pride in his ship. It is a great beauty with that mark of the perfect clipper ship: a magnificent curve to its bow. This curve provides the great speed for which the ship was built. It is trim, elegant and handsome; just like my Captain; a true Aristocrat of Sail.

"Clam Chowder"

Steam 2 quarts clams — save juices — shuck and cut into pieces. Fry salt pork in small pieces. Cook 3 small onions chopped up; salt and pepper to taste. Add 6–8 medium-sized potatoes cut up; add 2 cups of water; mix altogether until soft; then cook. Add clams, juice, 1 quart of milk; piece of butter the size of an egg; decorate with fresh parsley and serve with common crackers.

"Baked Indian Pudding"

1 quart sweet milk, scalding hot, and pour over 7 even tablespoonsful of Indian meal. 1 small teacup of molasses. Then add 1 cup of cold milk. Also ½ cup sultanas. Bake 3 hours in a deep dish.

"A Merry Heart"

Jog on, jog on, the footpath way,
   And merrily hent the stile-a;
A merry heart goes all the day,
   Your sad tires in a mile-a.

"A Winter's Tale"
Wm. Shakespeare

"Court of St. James Cake"

3 eggs
1 cup of new milk
1 cup of butter
2 cups of sugar
2 teaspoonsful cream of tartar
1 teaspoonful of soda
4 cups of flour

Bake in a medium oven about 1 hour. It makes two delicious loaves and it is the Captain's favourite cake.

o——◦◦◦◦◦◦◦◦◦◦◦◦◦◦◦◦◦◦◦◦◦◦◦◦◦◦◦◦◦◦◦◦◦◦◦◦

"Colonial Fruit Cake"

1 pound of flour
1 pound of sugar
10 ozs. butter
¼ pound of citron
¾ pound sultanas
6 eggs
Add a wineglass of milk.
Chop in orange, mace or nutmeg.

This receipt can take 7 eggs and save out 2 whites for frosting. Bake in medium oven 1¼ to 1½ hours.

"The Last Return from the Sea"

October 1, 1871

Today is the first day of October. It is a veritable gold and crimson fantasy as far as the eye can see. Such splendor, such magnificence: the golden sun rising from the smoke hazed mountains transforming them into a wonderland of riotous colours then continuing on in its orbit ever upward radiating in the vast heavens of cerulean blue.

I arose early this morning just as the mists were rising above the water and the sun was breaking through. All morning I felt a strange inner unrest, a feeling of unrestrained joy and expectation. Could this be the day? I carefully made my most perfect lemon meringue pie and then left it to cool. I hastily dressed in a soft emerald green velvet riding habit. I donned a tocque of green ostrich plumes and then set off on my favourite chestnut bay, Star. I called to Dutchess, the terrier and Moira and Rori, the Irish setters; we set off at a fairly brisk pace through the perfect wood down to the pond. There, rivulets of dew were evaporating in the warmth of the sun. The pond, so still, faithfully reflected the irridescent images of all that it captured within its depths: the trees, the leaves, the sun, the sky. Shy deer daintily sipped the cool water, joined by rabbits and an occasional mother fox and her pretty cubs. I had a basket with me containing bread for the fish, birds and animals and small treats for the horse, the dogs and myself. As the morning wore on, we walked further into the peaceful wood to the holy place my Captain and I had made. There by the small shrine to St. Francis, I knelt and prayed, "Please send my Captain safely

131

home, today." As I rose and turned, I thought I saw a vision, but no! There he was running to me through the wood, the sunlight catching the glint from his golden hair. I immediately ran to him with the dogs at my side barking for joy. It was as if we were in a dream. Then I was in his strong arms: that magic circle of love and contentment. My Captain lifted me onto the horse, took the reins, and we started home.

My Captain is home, nevermore to venture forth to sea. I will now be able to gaze at him to my heart's content, everyday. My love has returned. My life is complete.

"Jamaican Schrimp"

4 lbs. large Gulf schrimp. Cook about 3 lbs. large, ripe, juicy fresh tomatoes. Then puree them.

Add
1 ½ tsp. tumeric
1 tsp. coriander*
1 tsp. ginger
1 tsp. cumin*
red pepper to taste
salt to taste

Cook for about 20 minutes, in large pan. Serve with about 4 cups cooked rice. For a savoury, dip in English Gray's Chutney*.

The Captain brought this receipt back from Jamaica.

* See appendix.

"Raisin and Rhubarb Pie"

Clean rhubarb and cut up fine enough to fit your pie dish. Mix 3 tablespoonsful of flour with 1½ cups of sugar, scatter over rhubarb. Add 1½ cups plump raisins rolled in flour. Season with nutmeg. Bake in a hot oven for 40 min.

"Cider Pie"

Mrs. Spaulding's receipt

1 egg
1 cup sugar
1 heaping tablespoonful of flour
3 large tablespoonsful of cider

If this does not fill the crust, add water also lemon if you like. Beat this all together thoroughly. Dried apples, chopped can also be added. Bake until firm.

I think it is very good for a change and the Captain is very fond of it. His mother usually makes it for him when she visits for a while.

Christmas — December 25, 1871

I have been very busy preparing for this very special Christmas. I have been baking mince pies in the traditional shape of Mangers with tiny sugar replicas of the Christ Child on the tops; also Plum Puddings and special Christmas pies and candies.

I have been decorating the house with pungent pine and fir; garlands of laurel, holly and ivy. Draped over the many mantels will be garlands, scarlett ribbands, bayberry candles and silver candlesticks. Mistletoe will be hanging from the ceiling. The tree will be decorated on Christmas Eve; the Holy Scene will be set up in the alcove and the firelite and candlelite will illuminate everything.

I am so happy this Christmas because the Captain retired this year. He is in business with both our fathers and joy of joys — he is home for supper every night!

"Baked Indian Corn"

Mix 3 cups of cooked corn with 3 cups of milk, 3 beaten eggs, salt, ground pepper. Place in large baking dish; cover with buttered bread crumbs. Bake in a moderate oven for ½ hour.

I am fevered with the sunset,
I am fretful with the bay,
For the wander-thirst is on me
And my soul is in Cathay.
There's a schooner in the offing,
With her top-sails shot with fire,
And my heart has gone aboard her
For the Islands of Desire.
I must forth again tomorrokw!
With the sunset I must be,
Hull down on the trail of rapture
In the wonder of the Sea.

"Sponge Cake No. 2"

take 1½ cups sugar
3 fresh eggs — large
½ cup sweet milk — fresh
1½ cups flour
2 teaspoonsful cream of tartar
½ teaspoonful soda

"Song"

Thomas Hood

A lake and a fairy boat
To sail in the moonlight clear —
And merrily we would float
From the dragons that watch us here!
Thy gown should be snow-white silk,
And strings of orient pearls,
Like gossamers dipped in milk,
Should twine with thy coppery curls!
Red rubies should deck thy hands
And diamonds should be thy dower —
But fairies have broke their wands
And wishing has lost its power!

"A Song of Drake's Men"
Alfred Noyes

The moon is up: the stars are bright:
    The wind is fresh and free!
We're out to seek for gold tonight
    Across the silver sea!
The world was growing gray and old;
    Break out the sails again!
We're out to seek a Realm of gold
    Beyond the Spanish Main!

"Blanc Mange"
French

Pound in mortar ½ lb. blanched almonds; 3 to 4 tablespoonsful of butter; ¼ cup water; ½ cup milk. Mix together as much as is necessary to extract all flavor from almonds. Strain mixture through a clean, linen cloth. Meanwhile soak 1 tablespoonful gelatin in ¼ cup of water and heat until scalded in top of double-boiler, 1 cup of cream and ½ cup sugar. Add almond mixture and gelatin mixture. When cool, stir in 1 tablespoonful Kirsch. Chill for several hours and serve with fruit and frothy cream.

"Blueberry Cake"

1 cup molasses
2 cups flour
½ cup butter
2 eggs
nutmeg, cloves
1 cupful blueberries or raisins
1 teaspoonful soda
Bake 1 hour in a moderate oven.

"Roly, Poly Pudding"

Mix 8 oz. short bread dough. Roll out and spread with molasses. Sprinkle with ¼ lb. breadcrumbs, add 1 cup currants and sultanas mixed. Roll up and place on a baking sheet. Bake for 30 minutes till well-browned. Serve with custard sauce.

"Delmonico Pudding"

Scald a pint of milk, mix 3 tablespoonsful of cornstarch with a little cold milk, add the yolks of 2 eggs beaten with 4 tablespoonsful of sugar, a little salt. Stir these into the scalded milk stirring it until it thickens. Pour this into a pudding dish, flavor with vanilla, sit it in the oven — let it remain long enough to form a crust sufficient to hold the frosting. Beat the whites of the eggs to a stiff froth. Then stir in about two tablespoonsful of powdered sugar and a little vanilla. Spread this over the top and brown in the oven. To be eaten cold.

"Shopping List"

Boston, Massachusetts — September 21, 1872

1. Violet-blue merino wool for a walking suit with fur trim. (Ask Mrs. Nutting for yardages required and prices.)

2. New fur-lined cloak — opossum fur. Wine coloured velour. "Gorgeous!" the Captain's comment.

3. Gabrielle dress in wine colour to match the above. Satin trim, braid-soutache type in like colour.

4. Seal-skin sack.

5. Carriage blankets for the new Barouche. Also a fur Buffalo Robe.

6. An emerald-green Sacque.

7. 10 yds. China silk, seagreen @ $5. per yard $50.00

8. A new Water Colour Set and paper.

"Boston Baked Beans"

Soak 3 cups pea beans overnight in cold water on back of stove. Next morning, cover with fresh water and parboil until skins split. Cut up 3/4 lbs. salt pork and place at bottom of brown Rockingham pot. Cover with the beans. Add 1/3 – 1/2 cup molasses; 1/3 cup maple syrup; 2 teaspoonful salt, 1 teaspoonful dry mustard and work mixture together. Cover all with home-preserved tomatoe catsup. Cover and bake in slow oven most of the day, basting with catsup or water.

"Love Not Me"

Love not me for comely grace,
For my pleasing eye or face,
Nor for any outward part;
No nor for a constant heart!
For these may fail or turn to ill:
So thou and I shall sever.
Keep therefore a true woman's eye,
And love me still but know not why!
So hast thou the same season still
To doat upon me ever.

Who Ever Loved, That Loved Not at First Sight?

Today we celebrate our 17th Wedding Anniversary and we still share a deep and abiding love for one another.

"Love is Eternal"

"French Loaf Cake"

Mrs. Margaret Macy, Lenox, Mass.

5 cups powdered sugar
3 cups fresh butter
2 cups milk
6 eggs
10 cups sifted flour
3 nutmegs, ground
a small teaspoonful soda
1 pound sultanas
¼ pound citron

Stir the sugar and butter to a cream. Then add part of the flour with the milk, a little warm and the beaten yolks of the eggs. Then add the remainder of the flour, whites of the eggs well-beaten, the spice, wine and brandy; soda and add the fruit before putting into pans. Bake about an hour in a medium oven.

For my 13th birthday I was taken to Tremont Temple in Boston to hear the great "Swedish Nightengale," Jenny Lind sing. The date was Oct. 1, 1850. She was so thrilling. I always loved to sing but from that moment I knew I wanted to be a fine singer.

"Corn Chowder"

Cook 3 medium-sliced onions in butter until light brown. Cook 5 medium-sized potatoes. When cooked, drain and cube. Warm 1 quart milk and 1 cup heavy cream in a heavy kettle. Add the onion, potatoes and 2½ cups cooked corn. Add ¼ cup of butter, salt, pepper and fresh parsley.

"Grape Preserves"

Put the sugar on the stove and put the white of an egg and the shell in; let it simmer then skim it out and put in the grape skins. Put the insides in by themselves; let them boil soft. Then strain and add to the skins.

"Madiera Cake"

Mrs. Dickson's family receipt

Mix: ¾ lb. flour
      to ¾ lb. sugar
      ¾ lb. butter
      3 eggs
      1 teaspoonful baking powder
      lemon flavor

Beat butter until soft. Mix dry ingredients; add sugar to butter first then flour; eggs and mix altogether. Add lemon and bake about 1 hour in moderate oven.

A merry heart, doeth good like a medicine; but a broken spirit drieth the bones.

Proverbs 17:22

"Stewed Chicken and Dumplings"

Prepare 5–6 lbs. plump fowl, clean and place in a heavy, black kettle; add giblets and cover with boiling water; add carrots, onions, celery, salt, bay leaf, thyme and sage. Cover pot and simmer, about 2–4 hours. When almost done, drop biscuit dough parslied, in spoonsful on gently bubbling stew. Cover and steam for 15 minutes.

Mrs. Dickson's receipt

I remember my 17th birthday so well. My parents gave a lovely party for our family and friends. It was a beautiful fall evening and before the guests arrived my Captain took me into the music room and told me that my father had given his permission to ask me to marry him. I could barely speak but I quickly recovered and told him that I would be honored to be his wife. He took my hand and placed a lovely emerald ring with diamonds surrounding it on my finger. "Green, to match your eyes," he said. We sealed our promises with a kiss. I still hold the magic of that moment in my heart and my soul. The rest of the evening was a dream. We danced almost every dance together and when we were apart we longed to be together again. It is now 1878 and we both feel exactly the same.

"Old-Fashion Molasses Pie"

Take 5 eggs, beaten; add 2 cups Barbados molasses; 2 heaping tablespoonsful of fresh butter, melted, ½ tsp. salt; 1½ tsp. vanilla flavoring. Cream into a paste. Pour into an unbaked pie shell. Bake in a slow oven until firm, about one hour. Serve with frothy sweet cream.

When the wind is in the East,
'Tis neither good for man nor beast;
When the wind is in the North,
The skillful fisher goes not forth;
When the wind is in the South,
It blows the bait in the fishes mouth;
When the wind is in the West,
Then 'tis at the very best.

"Rain before seven. Clear by eleven."

"Sour-milk Doughnuts"

Mrs. Francis

Mix together 4 1/2 cups flour; 1 1/2 teaspoonsful soda; 1 1/2 teaspoonsful cream of tartar; 1 teaspoonful salt; 1/4 teaspoonful nutmeg. Add 1 1/4 cups of loaf sugar; 3 tablespoonsful soft lard; 1 cup sour milk and 3–4 eggs depending on size. Mix all and roll out about 1/4 inch thick; cut with cutter or glass. Cook in deep hot fat for 3 min.; first one side then the other side. Put on coarse, brown paper to drain. Serve with powdered sugar or cinnamon and ground loaf sugar mixed.

"May the love of Heaven ever be with you and may the angel of peace watch over you ever."

B.

"Delicious Pudding"

Bake common sponge cake in a flat-bottomed pudding dish. When desired for use cut it into sixths or eighths. Split each, butter them and return them to their places in baking dish. Make a custard with 4 eggs. Take a quart of milk; season and sweeten to the taste and pour it over the cake. Bake half an hour. The cake will swell and fill the custard.

"Baked Apples"

Core out some, hard, sweet apples; place in baking dish; add some water. Cover apples with Barbados sugar, butter and molasses; sprinkle with cinnamon, cloves and nutmeg. Bake in medium oven about 1 hour. Serve warm with whipped cream, sweetened to taste.

"Mulled Cider"

Take two quarts of sweet cider; 2/3 cup Barbados sugar; 6 whole cloves; 6 whole allspice; 4 sticks of cinnamon. Mix all ingredients in pan; place over low fire; boil, then simmer a few minutes; strain through a linen cloth. Serve in earthenware mugs.

"Fritters"

Cut up apples, peaches, apricots; remove stones; dip in batter and fry in deep fat about 3–4 minutes. Lay on brown paper to absorb grease and sprinkle with powdered sugar.

"First Rate"

"Mock Mince Pies"

1 cup water
1 cup molasses
1 cup granulated sugar
1 cup cider — vinegar
1 cup sultanas floured
4 common crackers
4 tablespoonsful butter
spices
3 eggs beaten
1 ½ cups brandy poured over all
Bake 1–1 ½ hours in slow oven until firm.

"Harrison Cake"

2 cups molasses
1 cup sugar
1 cup sour cream
1 teaspoon cloves
2 teaspoons saleratus
2 tea cups currants
1 cup butter

The butter should be cut small and put in a pan with the molasses; melt them and pour upon it 3 or 4 cups flour; then add the sugar and half the cream. Put the soda in the remainder. Add more flour to make thick as cup cake also spices and fruit. Bake in a medium oven for about 45–50 minutes.

"Cider Cake"

Mrs. Arad Wood's

4 oz. of fine sugar
8 oz. of flour
3 eggs
¼ lb. of butter
½ –1 whole grated nutmeg to your taste
1 teacupful sweet cider
1 teaspoonful of soda

Cream sugar, butter; add flour, soda, nutmeg. Pour over all beaten frothy cider. Mix altogether. Bake in shallow, well-spattered tin in a medium oven for about 45 minutes.

o———ᴄᴍᴍᴏ⊁

"Superior Custard"

Take 12 large fresh eggs and beat together with 2½ cups of loaf sugar; 1½ teaspoonful salt. Meanwhile, scald 9 cups of milk; add to egg mixture. Also 4 teaspoonful vanilla. Then pour into a large pudding pan; cover with fresh ground nutmeg. Put pan in large pan of hot water and place in medium oven about 1 hour. Cool and serve with frothy flavored cream.

o———ᴄᴍᴍᴏ⊁

"The Sea"

Lord Byron

And I have loved thee, Ocean! and
My joy of youthful sports was on thy breast to be
Borne, like thy bubbles onward.
From a boy I wantoned with thy breakers, they to me
Were a delight; and if the freshening sea
Made them a terror, 'twas a pleasing fear;
For I was as it were a child of Thee,
And trusted to thy billows far and near,
And laid my hand upon thy mane — as I do here.

"Pumpkin Bread"

Mrs. George Elliot's

2 ½ cups flour
1 ½ teaspoonsful soda
1 ½ teaspoonsful salt
½ teaspoonful cinnamon
½ teaspoonful cloves
½ teaspoonful allspice
½ teaspoonful nutmeg
½ cup Barbados molasses
3 eggs
2 cups fresh cooked pumpkin
2 ¼ cups brown Barbados sugar
¾ cup lard
1 cup prunes chopped and floured
1 cup chopped nuts
1 cup dates chopped and floured

Bake in greased tube pan mold in a medium oven for about 1 hour.

"My Captain's favourite"

"Brown Bread to Steam"

2 cups Indian meal
2 cups rye meal
1 cup flour
1 ½ cups molasses
1 teaspoonful soda
1 ½ pints milk or water
Steam at least 4 hours.

"Rye Muffins"

2 cups sour milk
1 cup molasses
3 cups rye meal
1 cup flour
2 eggs
1 teaspoonful soda
Bake in medium oven about 20–25 minutes.

"Succotash"

Scrape kernels from several ears of corn to make about 3 cups altogether. Add shell beans and cover with water and cook until beans are tender. Add more water if needed. Drain; add butter the size of an egg; ½ cup thick cream and keep hot until ready to serve.

"Witch's Charm"

The owl is abroad, the bat and the toad,
    And so is the cat-a-mountain;
The ant and the mole sit both in a hole,
    And the frog peeps out o' the fountain.
The dogs they do bay, and the timbrels play,
    The spindle is now a-turning;
The moon it is red, and the stars are fled,
    But all the sky is a-turning.

"Apple Dumplings"

Procure some good, juice, tart apples; core and pare them, and fill up their cores with sugar and a little powdered cinnamon. Then rub two tablespoonsful of lard or butter into 1 quart of flour; add a pinch of salt and mix to dough. First sift enough to roll out very soft with a cupful of sour milk, in which half a teaspoon of saleratus has been dissolved. Roll out the dough as for soda biscuits and spread over with melted butter; fold it on the side, roll; then again let stand in morning half an hour covered. Form into large pieces which will cover 1 apple. Put into a biscuit pan. When filled, pour melted butter on top of each, scatter sugar over all and bake an hour. Serve with cream and sugar.

"Sauce for Apple Dumplings"

1 teaspoonful of sugar, the grated pulp and juice of 1 lemon. Add beaten white of one egg, 3 tablespoonsful of boiling water, boil 3 minutes.

"Plumley's Fruit Cake"

1 cup of butter
1 cup of brown Barbados sugar
1 cup of fresh sweet milk
3 cups of flour
4 large eggs
1½ teaspoonsful of soda
2 lbs. of sultanas
Pound fine 1 nutmeg.

This makes 2 beautiful loaves. Bake in moderate oven about 1–1½ hrs.

"Prune Whip"

1 cup cooked, beaten prunes
½ cup of nuts, chopped
1 cup of prune juice
3 egg whites, beaten
1 tablespoonful cornstarch
⅓ cup of sugar

Cook juice, starch, sugar, salt until thick. Cool. Add egg whites, prunes. Cool some more, then serve with frothy cream.

"All Hallow's Pudding"

Butter a large baking dish. Cut up thick slices of 6–7 large cooking apples. Take 1½ cups flour; ¾ cup brown Barbados sugar and ¾ cup loaf sugar; 1½ teaspoonsful cinnamon; 1½ teaspoonsful ginger; 1½ teaspoonsful mace and 1½ teaspoonsful nutmeg. Mix together; add 2½ cups of milk, stir well and pour over the apples. Blend in 1 cup of butter. Mix all, bake in medium oven for about 2 hours. Stir. Cover with sauce.

From Ghoulies
And Ghosties
Long Leggitie Beasties
And Things That
Go Bump in the Night
Good Lord Deliver Us!

"Chocolate Cake"

Mrs. Pierce's

½ cup of butter
1½ cups sugar
2½ cups flour
½ cup milk
3 eggs
1½ teaspoonsful baking powder

Stir sugar and butter together, then milk & eggs; then the flour containing the baking powder. Then take 8 heaping tablespoonsful of chocolate, 5 tablespoonsful of sugar and 3 tablespoonsful of boiling milk. Stir to a cream, put all together and bake in a medium oven for 40–50 min.

"Delicious Apple Cake"

¾ cup lard
1½ cups granulated sugar
4 eggs
2½ cups of flour
1 teaspoonful of soda
1 teaspoonful cinnamon
¾ cup hot coffee
2 cups cut up yellow Sheepnose Apples*
½ cup chopped nuts

Bake in a medium oven about 40–50 min. Mix lard, sugar, eggs; add dry mixture, apples, nuts. Place in greased & floured pan and sprinkle brown sugar and cinnamon on top.

"Thanksgiving Pudding"

First served 1861
and
almost every Thanksgiving thereafter.
The Captain's mother's own receipt. "Delicious."

Take two dozen common crackers and soak in milk enough to cover them overnight. In the morning when reduced to a pulp add a little more milk; 10 eggs; a bowl of sugar; a piece of butter the size of an egg; a pound and a half of sultanas, assorted spices and salt and bake.

* See appendix.

"Pudding Sauce"

1 cup sugar
½ cup of butter
1 beaten egg
1 glass of wine
nutmeg

Beat well together; set over tea kettle of boiling water; beat it until it frothes.

"Pork Cake"

Cut up about a pound to a pound and a quarter of fat salt pork; pour 2 cups of boiling water and let it stand about 15 minutes. Sift 8 cups of flour; add 2 teaspoonsful soda & ½ teaspoonful salt; 2½ teaspoonsful cloves; 2½ teaspoonsful cinnamon; 2½ teaspoonsful allspice; 2½ teaspoonsful nutmeg; 2½ cups of floured sultanas. Beat 5 eggs; add 2 cups fine loaf sugar; 2 cups molasses and mix with dry mixture. Add 1 cup of currants to mixture or 1 cup of citron. Bake in medium oven for 1¼ to 1½ hours. It makes 4 loaves.

"Squash Pie or Pumpkin Pie"

Take 1½ cups cooked squash or pumpkin; add 1 cup of brown sugar; ½ teaspoon clove; 1 teaspoon ginger; 1 teaspoon cinnamon; ¼ teaspoon nutmeg; 1 teaspoon salt; 1 cup sweet milk; 3 beaten eggs. Add molasses to taste. Mix together and pour into a large unbaked pie shell and bake about 1 hour in a medium oven.

"Cream Sponge Cake No. 2"

1 cup sugar; 1 cup flour; 2 eggs beat and put in a teacup; fill the cup with sweet cream; 1 teaspoon cream of tartar; ½ teaspoon saleratus. Mix together and put in lemon flavoring. Bake in a medium oven 40–50 minutes.

"Drop Cake Cookies"

Mrs. Pierce's

½ cup butter
1 cup sugar
2/3 cup sweet milk
yolk of 1 egg
1 teaspoon soda
2 teaspoonsful of cream of tartar

The white of the egg well-beaten, should be put in before the flour. Rub butter, sugar and yolk to a cream then dissolve the soda in a teaspoonful of warm water and add the cream of tartar to 2 cups flour, well-heaped. Now put all the material together and stir enough to mix the flour in well. Drop on pans and just before putting in the oven, put a whole raisin in the center of each cooky.

"Very Fine Mince Meat"

Mrs. Dickson's family receipt

Boil two beef's tongues (perfectly fresh) and when cold skin and mince them including the fat about the roots. Mince also 1 pound of beef suet and mix it with the chopped tongues. Add four nutmegs, powdered. Two ounces powdered cinnamon and an onze* of powdered mace with a tablespoonful of powdered cloves. Pick clean, wash and dry three pounds of Zante currants. Seed and chop three pounds of raisins. Mix the fruit with the ingredients adding a pound of citron sliced and grated yellow rind and juice of three lemons or oranges. Sweeten this mixture with 2 pounds sugar and moisten it with a quart of Madiera wine and a quart of brandy. Having thoroughly minced the whole, pack it down hard into small stone jars covering them closely and pasting strong white paper over the lid. Do not add brandy till you take out the mince meat for use. It is better allowing three large apples per pint of meat. Whenever you take out mince meat, put some more brandy to the remainder.

"Old English Beefsteak Pie"

Cut beefsteak, about 1 ½ lbs. in small pieces, roll in flour, salt and pepper. Brown. Then add 3 ½ cups boiling water. Add slowly the rest of the flour and steak sauce. Cover and cook until tender. Add 1 ½ – 2 cups of potatoes uncooked and cut up small. Cook all 15 min. more. Pour mixture in greased baking pan. Put 1 large diced onion on the top. Cover with pastry and make openings for steam to escape. Bake in hot oven for ½ hour.

Thos Royal throne of kings, this scept'red isle
This earth of majesty, this seat of Mass,
This other Eden, demi-paradise,
This fortress built by Nature for herself
Against infection and the hand of war,
This happy breed of men, this little world,
This precious stone set in the silver sea.
This blessed plot, this earth, this realm, this England.

"Receipt for English Mead"

Mrs. B. F. Spaulding

2 pounds granulated sugar
1 pint of molasses
3 oz. of tartaric acid
essence of lemon
1 quart of water

Put 2 tablespoonsful in 1 glass of water and a quarter spoon of soda. Let it stand overnight. It is better.

Sing hey! Sing hey!
For Christmas Day.
Twine mistletoe and holly.
For friendship glows
In winter snows
And so let's all be jolly!

"Graham Cake"

2 ½ cups flour
1 cup sugar
1 cup sweet, fresh milk
1 large fresh egg
1 teaspoonful cream of tartar
1 teaspoonful soda
1 teaspoonful suet
1 large tablespoonful butter
Bake in moderate oven for about 50 minutes.

"Sponge Cake No. 3"

Break 2 eggs in a cup and fill it up with heavy cream.

1 cup sugar
1½ cups flour
1 teaspoonful cream of tartar
½ teaspoonful soda

Bake in medium oven 40–45 minutes. Fill with chocolate creme filling. Spread heavy frothy cream all over. Sprinkle with nuts.

"Superior."

"Cranberry Sauce"

Boil 1 quart fresh cranberries; add 2 cups loaf sugar; 1 cup sultanas; 1 cup water. Cut up 2 medium-sized fresh Seville oranges in small pieces. Leave rind on like you do for marmalade. Cook all until cranberries pop open. Store in covered crock.
"Delicious with meats, turkey and goose."

"Pudding Sauce"

Mrs. Pierce's

Put 1½ tablespoonsful of flour, well-beaten in cold water. Pour boiling water over flour mixture then put in a tablespoonful fresh butter. Beat an egg and ½ cup sugar together; strain the flour and water into the bowl with the egg and the sugar and flour.

"English Christmas Tea Cake"

2 cups flour
1 cup sugar
½ lb. butter
¼ tsp. salt
¼ tsp. mace
¼ teaspoon cream of tartar
1 lb. currants, floured
5 eggs, beaten
7 tablespoonsful brandy
Grease pan. Place in slow oven 1¼ hours.

Served for Christmas dinner on the "Clipper Ship" according to my great grandmother's receipt. She was Mrs. Rosalind Wood St. James. I am told she always baked at least 12 for the holidays, two of which were always presented to the bishop and 2 to our parish priest.

"Onion and Sage Dressing"

Mrs. Arad Wood's

Roll out 40–45 common pilot crackers. Chop up 4 2" slices of salt pork. Add 2 tsp. cloves; 2 tsp. cinnamon; 2 cups of sultanas; 3 teaspoonsful of sale; 6-8 links of sweet sausage, cut up and cooked and 6 small onions, sliced. Bind all with 4 eggs and broth. You may add either 1 cup walnuts or 1 cup chestnuts or for still another variation — ½ cup walnuts and ½ cup chestnuts.

"English Plum Pudding

Mix 1½ cups of hot milk and 1½ cups fine bread crumbs in a large bowl and let stand until cool. Separate 4 eggs and yolks, beaten, also ½ cup sugar. Chop up ¼ lb. dried figs, ¼ lb. citron and ½ lb. sultanas ½ flour well. Add ¼ cup wine; ½ lb. suet; 1 teaspoon nutmeg; 3/4 teaspoon cinnamon; ¼ teaspoon ground cloves; ¼ teaspoon ground mace; 1½ teaspoons salt. Beat the egg whites until they are stiff, and fold them into the mixture. Butter the inside of a large mold or tin. A Turk's Head Mold will do nicely. Fill it 2/3 full of pudding mixture and cover tightly with cover. Steam for 3 hours the day before using and for 1 hour on the day used. Before serving, pour ¼ cup brandy or rum over pudding and light. Serve pudding with hard sauce.

"Roast Beef"

Mrs. Holmes Thayer

Lay a large, 10–12 pound roast beef in a heavy, shallow roasting pan. Salt and pepper well (fresh ground pepper if possible), either before or after roasting meat. Cut small pieces of fresh salt pork and place over roast. Place in slow oven until done, about 5 hours or until done to your taste. Serve with Yorkshire Pudding, potatoes and onions, carrots added while roasting meat.

"English Trifle"

Mrs. Phillips

Have your 8–10 little sponge cakes baked already. Take out your best large cut-glass bowl. I use my favourite pin wheel and star pattern footed bowl.

Cut up sponge cakes and place them nicely in the bowl. Pour in enough sherry to soak them through. Have your favourite custard made and flavor it with sherry or brandy. Pour hot over the sponge cakes. When very cold, press whitened almonds thickly throughout. Add layer of thick whipped cream. (Use powdered type.) Decorate with more almonds and candied cherries.

"To be served especially on Christmas Day after a sumptuous dinner of roast turkey, roast beef, potatoes, glazed sweet potatoes, cranberry sauce, Chestnut stuffing, oysters, plum pudding with hard sauce, cakes and pies of every description."

Lines from Mr. Pickwick's
"Christmas at Dingley Dell"

Charles Dickens

A happy party they were that evening. The snow had begun to fall softly through a starlight night. Within, the best sitting room at Manor Farm was a good, long, dark-pannelled room with a high chimney-piece. At the upper end of the room seated in a shady bower of holly and evergreens were the two best fiddlers, and the only harp in all Muggleton. In all sorts of recesses and on all kinds of brackets stood massive old silver candlesticks with four branches each. The carpet was up, the candles burnt bright, the fire blazed and crackled on the hearth and merry voices and light-hearted laughter rang through the room.

When they were all tired of dancing, blindman's bluff and other games, there was a great game of snap-dragon, and when fingers enough were burned with that and all the raisins gone they sat down by the huge fire of flaming logs to a substantial supper of stout ale, roast goose, plum pudding, apples, toasted chestnuts, apple tarts, mince pie and a mighty silver bowl of Wassail in which the hot apples were hissing and bubbling with a rich look and a jolly sound, that was perfectly irresistable. Up flew the bright sparks in myriads as the logs were stirred and the deep red blaze sent forth a rich glow that penetrated into the furthest corner of the room, and cast its cheerful tint on every face. As the clock struck twelve and joyful Christmas was ushered in, every voice rose in happy song.

Author's Note

I have tried to keep the feeling of antiquity in this book so I copied every receipt exactly as is. However, since this cookbook was written at a time when fireplaces, ovens in chimneys and woodstoves were used for cooking, the times and temperatures will have to be gauged to your own stove and knowledge of similar receipts. I have found that slow ovens were about 325°, moderate or medium ovens between 350–375° and fast or hot oven between 400–425°. My stove is a gas stove and if you have an electric one it may respond differently.

Appendix

Alum — astringent roots of various plants

Barbados sugar — brown sugar

Bergamot — a wild mint

Cassia — a variety of cinnamon

Castor sugar — white, granulated sugar

Checkerberry — sweet berry for flavoring

Coriander — a plant, the fruit of which is aromatic

Cumin — an herb

Devil's Tongs — large pinchers to extract hard brown sugar from barrel

Extract of Rosé — made from rose petals

Gray's Chutney — famous English brand of savoury

Gum Arabic — gum exuded from the Acacia tree

Gum Dragon — another gum used as a binder

Hops — used to give bitter flavor to malt liquors

Horehound — an herb whose bitter juice is used as a cough medicine

Indian Meal — cornmeal

Isinglass — a very pure form of gelatin used for making jellies and clarifying liquors

Loaf sugar — white, refined sugar

Mace — a spice consisting of the dry, outer covering of the nutmeg

Onze — ounce

Pennyroyal — a species of mint with medicinal properties

Quassia Cup — wooden cup taken from the Quassia Tree — Whatever is placed in this cup takes on a special flavor.

Sago — a species of starch used in making puddings

Saleratus — baking soda

Senna — a shrub having medicinal properties for digestive problems

Sheepnose Apples — Delicious

Sultanas — yellow raisins

Tartaric Acid — potassium salt

Thoroughwart — an aromatic plant

Treacle — English word for molasses

Turmeric — the root from which curry powder is made

"Turk's Head" Mold — a nautical ornamental knot that resembles a turban. A
mold for puddings and cakes shaped this way.

Celtic — Irish

Grá — My love
A ghrá — My husband
A captáen — My captain

Index

Puddings (continued)

Rice

Sauces

Vegetable Dishes

The Captain's Lady Collections

**65-69 HIGH STREET
SPRINGFIELD, MASSACHUSETTS 01105**

Send me _____ copies of your book at $10.95.
Please make checks payable to The Captain's Lady Collections.

Name _____

Street _____

City _____ State _____ Zip _____

- -

The Captain's Lady Collections

**65-69 HIGH STREET
SPRINGFIELD, MASSACHUSETTS 01105**

Send me _____ copies of your book at $10.95.
Please make checks payable to The Captain's Lady Collections.

Name _____

Street _____

City _____ State _____ Zip _____

- -

The Captain's Lady Collections

**65-69 HIGH STREET
SPRINGFIELD, MASSACHUSETTS 01105**

Send me _____ copies of your book at $10.95.
Please make checks payable to The Captain's Lady Collections.

Name _____

Street _____

City _____ State _____ Zip _____

The Captain's Lady Collections

65-69 HIGH STREET
SPRINGFIELD, MASSACHUSETTS 01105

Send me _____ copies of your book at $10.95.
Please make checks payable to The Captain's Lady Collections.

Name _____

Street _____

City _____ State _____ Zip _____

- -

The Captain's Lady Collections

65-69 HIGH STREET
SPRINGFIELD, MASSACHUSETTS 01105

Send me _____ copies of your book at $10.95.
Please make checks payable to The Captain's Lady Collections.

Name _____

Street _____

City _____ State _____ Zip _____

- -

The Captain's Lady Collections

65-69 HIGH STREET
SPRINGFIELD, MASSACHUSETTS 01105

Send me _____ copies of your book at $10.95.
Please make checks payable to The Captain's Lady Collections.

Name _____

Street _____

City _____ State _____ Zip _____